6/20

F:
6/30/20

A Different Kind of Poison
How Legalism Destroys Grace
Kevin Pendergrass

All Scripture quotations, unless otherwise indicated, are taken from the Holy Bible, New International Version®, NIV®. Copyright ©1973, 1978, 1984, 2011 by Biblica, Inc.™ Used by permission of Zondervan. All rights reserved worldwide. www.zondervan.com. The "NIV" and "New International Version" are trademarks registered in the United States. Patent and Trademark Office by Biblica, Inc.™

Copyright 2018 Kevin Pendergrass

All rights reserved. No part of this book may be reproduced or transmitted in any form or by any means without written permission from the author, except for the inclusion of brief quotations in articles and reviews. For information, contact Kevin Pendergrass at kevin@kevinpendergrass.com
Printed and Bound in the United States of America

Book layout and formatting by Daniel Rogers. For self-publishing services and consultation, visit http://danielrogers.us.

Acknowledgements

Thank you to everyone who made this endeavor possible and to those who helped with editing this work. A special thanks to Daniel Rogers who gave me the encouragement to go ahead and write the book. Daniel, I appreciate your friendship. Thank you for the effort you put into formatting this book and getting it ready to be published.

Dedication

God has blessed me with the most wonderful wife. Without my beautiful and God-fearing wife, Bethany, I wouldn't be where I am today. God brought you into my life at the perfect time and we have learned so much together. Thank you for being my rock in life.

To my parents, thank you so much for always being there and supporting me. You were the ones who taught me what it means to trust God in the good times and the bad times.

God has also blessed me with two best friends who are closer to me than brothers. Brandon Johnson and Terry Patterson, you guys mean the world to me. I wouldn't be me without your guidance, advice, and love.

Table of Contents

Acknowledgements iii
Dedication iii
Table of Contents iv
Foreword vii

PART 1: INTRODUCTION 1
   THE OBJECTIVE 3
   WHAT IS LEGALISM? 7
   HOW LEGALISM IS A POISON 9
   WHY LEGALISM IS A DIFFERENT KIND OF POISON . 11

PART 2: MY EARLY CHILDHOOD 13
   PICTURE-PERFECT WORLD 15
   WHEN TRAGEDY STRIKES 19
   DEATH BECOMES A REALITY 21

PART 3: MIDDLE SCHOOL AND HIGH SCHOOL 25
   YOUTHFUL ZEAL 27
   JUST LIKE ME 29
   A NEW FRIENDSHIP 33
   OVER-INFLATED EGO 37

PART 4: LIFE IN PREACHING SCHOOL 41
   A NEW JOURNEY BEGINS 43
   WALK THE WALK 45
   STANDING MY GROUND 49
   SAME SONG, DIFFERENT VERSE 51

PART 5: MINISTRY OF MASS DESTRUCTION 53
   MY CAREER TAKES OFF 55
   DISTORTED VIEW OF OTHERS 59
   TURNING THE TABLES 63
   TAKE IT OUTSIDE 65

DISRESPECT..67
CHURCH CRASHERS..69

PART 6: A DANGEROUS MENTALITY............................**73**
CONFIRMATION BIAS 75
BELIEF PERSEVERANCE..79
A CHINK IN MY ARMOR 83

PART 7: RE-EXAMINING MY APPROACH TOWARD OTHERS...**87**
AM I BEING CONSISTENT?..89
CHECKING MY MOTIVATION 93
STILL THE SAME 97

PART 8: THE QUESTIONS BEGIN **99**
FELLOWSHIP: PARTY OF ONE......................................101
UNDERTONES OF ASCETICISM....................................107
WHAT IS SIN? 111
WRONG, BUT NOT SIN 113
THE GOLDILOCKS COMPLEX.......................................117

PART 9: LIVING IN FEAR **121**
FEAR OF BEING WRONG 123
BLURRED VISION 129
I RESIGN FROM MY JOB 133
LOSING MY IDENTITY 137

PART 10: BACK TO THE FUNDAMENTALS **139**
UNDERSTANDING GOD'S HOLINESS AND LOVE 141
THE GOSPEL 145
IS HEAVEN REALLY THAT SMALL? 149
USING THE LAW LAWFULLY 153
NOT ENOUGH POINTS 159
ACCESSING GOD'S GRACE 163
BUT WHAT ABOUT WORKS? 167

PART 11: CONNECTING THE DOTS 173
    IN SEARCH OF A PERFECT LOVE 175
    CONTRARY TO THE LAW 181
    DOES GOD CONTRADICT HIMSELF? 185
    LISTEN TO OUR HEARTS 189
    GOD'S GRACE AND MY IGNORANCE 195

PART 12: THE CHANGE 199
    THE MOST IMPORTANT CHAPTER 201
    THE WILL OF GOD: KNOWING JESUS 207
    RELATIONAL ILLUSTRATIONS 211
    MY APPROACH TO GOD 217
    MY APPROACH TO SCRIPTURE 219
    MY APPROACH TO UNITY AND FELLOWSHIP 225

PART 13: CONCLUSION 233
    ALREADY LEFT LEGALISM? 235
    IN THE PROCESS OF LEAVING LEGALISM? 239
    THINKING ABOUT LEAVING LEGALISM? 243
    FINDING YOUR OWN FAITH 247

Foreword

I have discovered that major life events are best traversed with a good friend by your side. God blesses some of us with friends to walk with us through those difficult and stressful moments of life. These friends pick us up when we fall, encourage us when we feel like quitting, and sometimes give us a swift kick to bring us back to reality.

God has blessed me with such a friend and you are about to embark on his story. Kevin is one of those truly rare people who "what you see is what you get." He possesses a rare combination of acute logic and reasoning skills, unwavering commitment to his convictions, and an unquenchable desire to search out the truth.

A Different Kind of Poison: How Legalism Destroys Grace will captivate you. The story is compelling, but this is more than a great story. It's a concise demonstration of how we can poison the greatest gift that has ever been given - the grace of Jesus Christ. There are many who have walked the path of legalism, but few know its depths, deception, and destruction more than Kevin.

Having practiced, preached, and publicly defended a system that destroys grace, he is uniquely able to demonstrate how we can get sucked in without realizing it. In *A Different Kind of Poison: How Legalism Destroys Grace*, Kevin slowly strips away the covers of legalism by telling his story and sharing his own struggle with attempting to reconcile the teachings of Jesus with his long-entrenched convictions. You will laugh, cry, and likely be challenged as you progress through the pages of this book.

Your time is valuable. Should you spend it reading a book about this subject? The answer is a loud and clear "YES!" I say this for two reasons.

First, as a man who was raised on legalism and preached it for years, I can personally attest to the reality of the destruction caused by it. I have seen close families torn apart, churches full of people that claim to follow Jesus fracture and never recover, the closest of friends alienated from each other, and people quit Jesus altogether because of legalism. I have personally experienced many of these in my own life. The damage is real, and the people are real. Those who are hurt by their own legalism or that of others are left scarred for years and in some cases forever.

Secondly, this subject deserves attention because people like Jesus, Paul, Peter, John, and others in the Bible thought it deserved attention. Some of Jesus' biggest adversaries were the Pharisees. Their problem was legalism. A large portion of Paul's letters, including most of Romans and Galatians, address legalism. In Acts chapter 15, Peter and others spoke to refute the principles of legalism. Yes, this book is meaningful and relevant to 21st Century followers of Jesus.

Satan has many tools in his bag. He knows how to find our weaknesses and exploit them. He does not show up and say, "Hi, I'm the devil and I'm here to tempt you." He is subtle. He is patient. He is deceptive. He knows how to poison the hearts of people. One of his most tried and proven poisons is legalism. This book will help you discover how to identify legalism and how to overcome it. I now invite you to sit back, delve into Kevin's story, and see why legalism is truly a different kind of poison.

Brandon Johnson

Minister

Part 1: Introduction

CHAPTER 1
The Objective

I want to personally thank you for being interested in my story. I am sincerely humbled and honored that you have chosen to read my book. I ask that you consider the things that you are about to read prayerfully, with an open heart, an open mind, and an open Bible. It is my hope that my story will challenge you, encourage you, and ultimately draw you closer to Jesus in a humble and confident faith.

We all have stories. While each one is unique, I have found that we, as humans, aren't so different after all. Stories are powerful because they help us relate to one another. They give us background and context.

When Paul the apostle was on trial, he told his story about his spiritual journey (Acts 22:1-21; 26:12-23). He began by telling them about the man he used to be and then explained why he changed his life. This book is my attempt to do the same thing.

If you had told me when I was younger that one day I would be writing a book about how my entire approach to Christianity changed, I would have thought you were crazy. I once thought I had all the answers and knew everything there was to know about God and the Bible. Needless to say, I was in for a rude, but much needed, awakening.

This book is not some better-felt-than-told story. I didn't have a miraculous revelation while driving down the road. God didn't visit me in a dream and He didn't come to my house to have a special conversation with me. On the contrary, it was through continual study of the Bible, humbling experiences, prayer, and honest reflection that God led me to understand more fully my own shortcomings, my desperate need for His grace, and the realization that I had been approaching Christianity incorrectly.

As you read, you will notice I have avoided discussing specific church affiliations and doctrines. I try to be as vague as possible when referencing some of my specific changes about different topics because those specifics are not the focus of the book.

The point of this book is to discuss why a legalistic approach to our faith is faulty while, at the same time, exploring the proper approach toward Christianity and the Bible.

The erroneous approach to Christianity that I used for many years is not limited to certain doctrines or church affiliations. It can be used by any church, at any time, by any person, and with virtually any conceivable issue.

While I am very open about the specific doctrines on which I have changed and have written extensively about them, it is not in the scope of this book to address those issues. Instead, this book will be much more applicable since what I will be discussing can affect everyone in Christendom.

There are also certain stories that I will tell of my encounters with others. In some of these examples, I will use real names where I have been granted permission. In other instances, I have changed the names out of courtesy and to protect the privacy of others. When I do assign a different name to someone, it will be noted with quotations the first time it is used.

For years, I was a Christian living in spiritual bondage without realizing it. I made so many mistakes and robbed myself of spiritual peace, joy, and freedom. I unintentionally hurt myself and others in the name of Jesus.

I don't want you to make the same mistakes. However, if you have already made some of those mistakes, that is OK since this book is not only about prevention, but also transformation.

My objective for writing this book is to explain how dangerous legalism is while providing ways to identify, combat, overcome, and prevent it in the future. However, first it is important that we are on the same page about the proper meaning of the term. So, what exactly is legalism?

CHAPTER 2
WHAT IS LEGALISM?

Before we get started on this journey, it is essential that I define exactly what I mean when I use the word legalism. I have found that this term is often thrown around haphazardly with little respect to the actual meaning of the word itself.

The meaning of legalism is simply "the doctrine that salvation is gained through good works."[1] Many believe that Edward Fisher first coined this English term around 1645.[2] Paul used the root word for legalism when teaching against salvation by works.[3] When Paul wrote to the Christians in Galatia who were caught up in attempting to be justified by the law, he said:

> ...know that a person is not justified by the works of the law, but by faith in Jesus Christ. So we, too, have put our faith in Christ Jesus that we may be justified by faith in Christ and not by the works of the law, because by the works of the law no one will be justified. (Gal. 2:16).

When commenting on Gal. 2:16 and the word "law," Ernest De Witt Burton said that Paul is "denoting divine law viewed as a purely legalistic system made up of statutes, on the basis of obedience or disobedience to which individuals are approved or condemned as a matter of debt without grace."[4] Paul taught that

---

[1] www.dictionary.com, "Legalism." This is the first theological definition given. It is the proper and accepted understanding in Christendom.
[2] Fisher, Edward. *The Marrow of Modern Divinity*.
[3] www.biblehub.com/greek/3551.htm, 3551. "Nomos."
[4] Burton, Ernest De Witt. *The International Critical Commentary:*

legalism shouldn't be viewed through a limited scope. He made the point that, while attempting to be saved through the Old Testament law is legalism[5], attempting to be saved through *any* law system is also legalism. This is such an important fact to understand. This is made clear when Paul said:

> ...if a law had been given that could impart life, then righteousness would certainly have come by the law. (Gal. 3:21).

Furthermore, when Paul condemned justification by law in Rom. 1-5, he didn't limit his usage to just the Old Testament law. He spoke about the law of the Gentiles and the law of which Abraham was amenable. The law of the Gentiles was separate from the law of Moses (Gal. 2:14-15) and the law that Abraham was under predated the law of Moses (Rom. 4:13; Gal. 3:15-18).

Please understand that obedience to God is *not* legalism (Heb. 5:8-9; 1 Jn. 5:3).[6] Teaching that the Bible is the objective standard of right and wrong is *not* legalism (2 Tim. 3:16-17; Jn. 8:32).[7] Teaching against sin is *not* legalism (2 Tim. 4:3). Holding other Christians accountable is *not* legalism (Heb. 3:12-13). Emphasizing the whole counsel of God is *not* legalism (Acts 20:20, 27). On the contrary, legalism happens when one attempts to be justified through *any* works/law-based system.

Clearly, trying to be saved through our own works is a faulty way to view Christianity. You may even be asking yourself how any Christian could ever view Christianity through the lenses of legalism. However, one of the fundamental dangers with legalism is that no one wants to believe they are infected with it.

Galatians, 1921, p. 120.
[5] Rom. 9:31-32; Gal. 5:4; Jn. 1:17; Rom. 3:28; Phil. 3:9
[6] Jn. 14:15; 15:14; 2 Jn. 6; Rev. 14:12
[7] Isa. 5:20; Rom. 10:17

CHAPTER 3
HOW LEGALISM IS A POISON

When I viewed Christianity through the framework of legalism, I had no idea that was what I was actually doing. I didn't wake up one morning and say, "Today, I want to attempt to earn my way to heaven." It didn't happen like that. It never happens like that. I am sure we would agree that would be silly. Legalism doesn't work that way.

In fact, on several occasions, I *was* accused of being a "legalist." Of course, I denied such at the time. I used to say that I would rather stand before God as "legal" than "illegal" any day.

So, if you're reading this and are thinking to yourself, "Kevin, I don't have a problem with legalism. I don't believe I can earn my way to heaven," then please keep reading this book. You see, I didn't think I had a problem with legalism, either.

I certainly never would have thought I actually believed I could earn my way to heaven. No Christian wants to believe they are adhering to a works-based salvation. While I always believed that I was *not* justified by law, my actions and application of my beliefs proved otherwise.

Somewhere along the way while striving to follow God, I got caught up in legalism. I never meant for it to happen. It was never part of the plan. The thought alone would have offended me. Yet, unbeknownst to me, I was attempting to earn my salvation.

So, why do I call legalism a "poison?" When I was in grade school, a firefighter came to speak to our class about the dangers of a certain poison known as carbon monoxide. He called this poison a silent killer. He told us that carbon monoxide has no taste, smell, or color making it difficult to detect until the effects have already manifested.[8]

Technically speaking, a poison is "any substance that through its chemical action usually kills, injures, or impairs an organism."[9] Poisons manifest themselves in diverse ways and can have varying effects on people's lives.

Spiritually speaking, legalism impairs, injures, and can even destroy us in different ways. Legalism causes people to trust in themselves without realizing it. The emphasis is placed on the individual and their work instead of God and His work.

When fully manifested, legalism ultimately destroys grace. Salvation by law doesn't give life; it takes it away (1 Cor. 15:56; 2 Cor. 3:6-18). When dealing with justification and salvation, Paul said:

> And if by grace, then it is no longer of works; otherwise grace is no longer grace. But if it is of works, it is no longer grace; otherwise work is no longer work. (Rom. 11:6).[10]

Similar to carbon monoxide, those influenced by legalism won't realize it until the symptoms have consumed their life in one sense or another. Legalism is not just a poison; it is a different kind of poison. In the next chapter, I will explain why this is the case.

---

[8] www.cbc.ca/news/canada/carbon-monoxide-poisoning-5-things-to-know-about-the-silent-killer-1.2575563. *Carbon monoxide poisoning: 5 Things to Know About The 'Silent Killer'*. CBC News. March 17th, 2014.
[9] www.merriam-webster.com/dictionary/poison
[10] NKJV

CHAPTER 4
WHY LEGALISM IS A DIFFERENT KIND OF POISON

At this point, you should already understand several things.

1. You should understand that legalism is when we view Christianity through the framework of a legal system and attempt to earn salvation through our own works.

2. You should understand that legalism isn't limited to any one church or issue. Rather, it is a mindset and an approach.

3. You should understand that those infected with legalism do not realize it. They do not believe they are actually trying to earn their way to heaven.

With these things in mind, I want to explain why legalism is a *different* kind of poison. I say that legalism is a different kind of poison because it is often worn by Christians who have good hearts and the best of intentions. They are usually good people, not bad. At first, they are well intended, not ill willed.

Most people involved in legalism are sincere and believe they are following the Bible. In fact, they probably are in many ways. They see themselves as obedient Christians who are only trying to follow God. Their actions are not done in the name of evil, but in the name of good. This was my experience, and this is what makes legalism so dangerous.

Unlike identifying a certain teaching, legalism is different because it is an approach and a mindset. There is no class called "How to Be a Legalist." Instead, it is naturally manifested any time someone acts on the belief that one is saved based upon their own works or merit.

I would like to point out here that there are many different symptoms and manifestations of legalism. Similar to any other poison, there will be varying effects. Therefore, in this book I will often refer to *my* specific symptoms.

Although the "symptoms" will vary from person to person, I have found that the specific manifestations of legalism that I will discuss in this book are very prominent and common among those infected with legalism.

So, what caused me to change my ways? What caused me to reconsider my approach? These questions and more will be answered throughout the book. For now, suffice it to say, I didn't change or even consider changing until the effects and symptoms of legalism were clearly and undeniably set before me.

Legalism had to manifest itself in multiple ways in my life before I came face to face with the realization that I was teaching and trying to live out a works-based system.

I saw it wasn't just about one or two biblical issues; it was about my whole approach to God. It was about my approach to Scripture. It was about my approach to people. It was how I was applying the Bible. Legalism impacts everything. If you don't believe me, then you will soon find out the truth as you read my story.

PART 2:
MY EARLY CHILDHOOD

CHAPTER 5
PICTURE-PERFECT WORLD

If I am going to tell you my story, what better place to start than the beginning? From birth, I was raised in a Christian environment. I have the most wonderful family in the world. To this day, I am extremely close to them. I believe I had the best childhood any kid could have filled with countless, wonderful memories.

Some of these memories include playing basketball with my dad, watching movies and playing mini golf with my mom, and going swimming in the summer or playing in the snow in the winter with my older sister. I remember our family building forts in the living room and watching TV shows like *Full House* and *America's Funniest Home Videos*. I wouldn't change my early childhood for anything.

We lived in a neighborhood full of children. The only problem was that I was the only boy. My sister, Kimberly, had several friends her age in the neighborhood and I was the annoying little brother that always caused them fits. Needless to say, I had a fun time getting them in trouble. It was what I lived for back then.

I was loved, and I knew it. As a child, I had a father, a mother, a sister, and grandparents who all loved me. They didn't just say they loved me, they showed it. Growing up, I assumed this was the norm for every kid. I am thankful that I was raised in a family where I learned about Jesus and the importance of the Bible. God was talked about daily and we wouldn't dare take a bite of dinner before Dad said a prayer.

As a young child, I enjoyed the different events and ministries offered by our church. The church I grew up in was fairly large and we always had fantastic Vacation Bible Schools and many other events, especially for children. My sister and I loved going to church and we had many friends there. Our family always went to gospel meetings, singings, and revivals whenever possible. We would go to almost every function conducted by our church.

Our congregation was very active and there constantly seemed to be some event going on in which everyone could be involved. It was my safe haven and I always looked forward to what was next. The young men were trained to be preachers, worship leaders, and song leaders. Our Bible classes were very elaborate, and we memorized Scripture every week.

There was a big event we participated in every year called Bible Bowl. It was a Bible competition with other churches where our knowledge was tested through a series of questions. We had a great team and usually won. I even had the certificates and trophies to prove it. I took great pride in that.

We also had a day camp during the summer. It was a fun week of learning how to read Scripture, lead singing, and even give a lesson in front of an audience. At the end of the week, we were all able to get up in front of the church and lead worship. That was a really neat thing for an elementary student.

As far as education was concerned, I grew up attending a private Christian school where we had daily devotionals and Bible classes. As I grew into my early tweens, I continued to have a growing interest in God and the Bible. I became a Christian at age 12 and I was on fire for the Lord.

Do you remember when the "WWJD" (What Would Jesus Do) bracelets were popular? I had several of those. I also bought shirts that had Bible verses on them and I would wear them proudly. As a kid, I just loved life. I was the class clown and loved making others laugh. If ever there was a picture-perfect childhood, I believe I lived it. However, when I was 13, little did I know something was about to happen that would change my life forever.

CHAPTER 6
WHEN TRAGEDY STRIKES

It was a Friday afternoon in August and school had just started back. I was in the 8th grade and my sister was a senior. At the time, we were at different schools. My mom had already picked me up from school and brought me back to our house.

I was lying on the couch watching TV while waiting for my friend, "James," and his mother, "Ms. Miller," to pick me up so I could spend the night with him.

I was looking forward to the weekend. James and I had a fun and busy weekend planned. We were both already tired of school and the next few days were going to be a nice break from reality.

While I was waiting for James and Ms. Miller to pick me up, the phone rang at our house and my mom answered. A few moments later, she walked into the living room and told me that Kimberly, my sister, had just been in a car wreck.

She was on her way home from school after volleyball practice and she was hit from behind by a pick-up truck. At the time, I was thinking it was just a fender bender. From all indications, I didn't think this was anything too serious.

My mom said she needed to meet my dad at the hospital and check on Kimberly. Being a typical 13-year-old, I asked her if I could just wait on James and Ms. Miller since they were almost there. Besides, in my mind, I wasn't going to let Kimberly ruin my weekend.

My mom agreed and told me that she would call me later at James' house to give me an update. I didn't even think twice about the situation. I knew of people who had been in car wrecks and it wasn't a big deal. There was no reason for me to believe this was any different.

Once I got to James' house, it wasn't but 30 minutes or so before Ms. Miller told me that my mom was on the phone and needed to talk with me. When I spoke with my mom, she didn't sound anxious. My mom has a way of staying very calm in difficult situations.

She told me in a very matter-of-fact way that I needed to come to the hospital. I started to complain and told her I didn't want to come to the hospital. I wanted to stay with James and have fun with my friend. Instead of Mom arguing with me, she just told me again that I needed to come to the hospital.

I asked Mom if I could just talk to Kimberly on the phone instead. I was going to give her a hard time for wrecking her new car. Plus, I figured if I could talk to Kimberly on the phone, that would pacify my mom and she wouldn't make me go to the hospital. I was focused on getting back to hanging out with James and doing more important things.

Instead of handing Kimberly the phone, my mom said that Kimberly couldn't talk right now and that I just needed to come to the hospital. You would think intuition would have kicked in at this point. However, I still didn't realize the seriousness of the situation.

As soon as I hung up the phone, Ms. Miller, James, and I went to the hospital. I remember Ms. Miller telling me how much she loved me and that everything was going to be OK. I thought her sentiments were odd because I didn't have a reason for everything not to be OK. However, I would soon find out that everything was not going to be OK.

CHAPTER 7
DEATH BECOMES A REALITY

When we arrived at the waiting room in the hospital, Kimberly's friends were there, many of my friends were there, and I recognized other acquaintances from church and school who were there. They were all crying and looked so sad. If you have ever had a surprise party, it was that kind of feeling except with all the good taken out of it.

I naturally asked several of my friends what they were doing there. No one would tell me what was happening. Before I could ask too many questions, one of the nurses escorted me to my family where they were waiting in a private room. They were crying, too. I just remember asking if someone could tell me what was going on with my sister.

My family hugged me, kept crying, and through their tears, I heard the simple and straightforward truth. They told me Kimberly was unconscious and she probably wasn't going to live much longer. I remember the surreal feeling when I heard those words. I couldn't even comprehend it. I had just seen her that morning. She was perfectly fine and now I am being told that she may not live through the night.

I had no time to even think about it. There was no time to prepare for it. The thought of my sister dying was a nearly impossible thought to understand for a 13-year-old.

The doctor who was overseeing my sister was a personal friend of ours. He had been waiting for me to arrive so he could talk to all of the immediate family at once. He told us he had never seen anyone survive with that much severe brain damage and even if she did survive, she would likely be in a vegetative state the rest of her life. He said that, medically speaking, there was a zero percent chance of her surviving through the night and we needed to prepare for her death.

There was so much information I was receiving at one time. I remember going to bed that night and waking up the next morning thinking everything had been a dream. Unfortunately, it wasn't a dream and the doctor would be correct in his assessment.

Within less than 24 hours of the wreck, my sister was pronounced dead on Saturday, August 21, 1999. I couldn't believe it. How could my sister be dead? How and why did this happen to her? What will this mean going forward? How will this change things?

I wanted to speak at Kimberly's funeral because I felt like it was the last thing I could do for her. There were many speakers that day at the funeral and over 1,000 people in attendance. I spoke for just a few minutes and told some funny stories about Kimberly and me.

I always liked being the comic relief and I knew Kimberly would have had it no other way. After the funeral was over, I knew things would be different, but I didn't realize how different.

Other people moved on with life, but Kimberly was still gone. Things had changed forever for us as a family. Yet, we learned to keep on going through life. Looking back, I am so thankful for my mom and dad who had, and still have, such great faith in God. Tragedy like this will either break you completely or make you into something greater. We allowed it to do the latter.

Through this tragedy, we became even closer as a family. I saw the reality of death and the certainty of it at a young age. Kimberly was just 17. In fact, she had just turned 17 a couple of months prior to her death. After she died, I started to take the concept of death seriously.

I never doubted God through that event. Rather, this made me realize how life is truly a vapor (Ja. 4:13-14). I saw up close that we can die at any time and we better be ready to meet God. The death of my sister instilled such a fear in me, though. Because of this fear, I wanted to make sure I was always ready to meet God if I were to die unexpectedly.

As with any human, the early years of life serve as a springboard to the future. I was going to take life (and death) very seriously now. The death of my sister brought to the surface some important questions: Who am I and who do I want to be in life? When will I die and how do I know I am going to heaven?

Part 3:
MIDDLE SCHOOL AND HIGH SCHOOL

CHAPTER 8
YOUTHFUL ZEAL

I was determined to be the absolute best Christian I could be after Kimberly died. While many of my friends were sowing their "wild oats" and living not-so-moral lives, I prided myself on how I was a faithful Christian. This is when my legalism really started.

Let me pause here and ask this question: How does someone become infected with legalism? Just like with any poison, you must first be exposed to it. Looking back, I can now see that the particular church where I grew up at had several people in their leadership who were very legalistic in their thinking. Of course, at the time, I didn't know anything different.

When we are young, we tend to see the whole world only through the lenses of our own experiences. Furthermore, I naturally accepted what I was taught since young children haven't mastered the art of critical thinking.

As a young Christian, I found myself being overly critical and judgmental of others. For example, if a student cussed, I would tell them straight to their face they were going to hell if they didn't repent of their sin.

I remember one time a guy named "Craig" talked about how he skipped church in order to go fishing with his older friends. I told him he would be fishing in the lake of fire one day if he didn't change his ways.

I engaged in these types of so-called "rebukes" all the time. Even though I went to a Christian school, most of the behavior by the students was not Christlike. I started to look down on others since I felt like I was one of the few living out my faith.

I never had a rebellious period in my youth and this naturally led me to believe I was a "better" Christian than others. This isn't to say I didn't have my own struggles or that I was perfect by any means, but I found my righteousness (or should I say self-righteousness) in abstaining from the typical vices of high school.

I never drank, I never did drugs, I never went to bad parties, I chose abstinence in my relationships, and I studied the Bible with anyone who was willing.

Regrettably, my Bible studies consisted of me telling everyone how wrong they were, how right I was, and how they needed to repent. I didn't take the time to show any patience, grace, or mercy, much less consider if I was wrong.

Even the times when I was right, I didn't handle it in the right spirit. I would later find out that some of the "worst kids" in my classes were raised in horrible circumstances that I didn't even know existed, such as having abusive parents.

Instead of taking the time to invest in their lives, befriend them, and show them Jesus, they only received judgment and condemnation from me.

However, I wouldn't just go after the "bad kids," I would also go after other Christians who didn't do Christianity just like I did it. No one was off limits. In order to be within my circle of friends, you had to be just like me.

CHAPTER 9
JUST LIKE ME

In my early teens, I was already becoming very dogmatic about the specific views of my church affiliation. If someone's church affiliation or congregation disagreed with mine, then I didn't mind telling them they were "wrong."

In one of our Bible classes at school, I got into a heated debate with another Christian named "Amber." At the time, Amber and I were discussing some petty differences between our views on a Bible subject.

I haughtily told her in front of the whole class she was wrong and she was going to go to hell if she didn't repent and change her views on certain subjects (As you can see, my pattern was to condemn people to hell right on the spot).

She was a great Christian girl, but she didn't believe everything just like I believed it. Therefore, I saw Amber as being condemned and I wasn't afraid to tell her.

During this time, I not only cut myself off from those who were choosing to live immoral lives, but I also cut myself off from Amber and others who didn't do Christianity just like me. This made it extremely hard to find friends.

My unintentional self-righteousness caused me to believe I was one of the only people who even cared about God. I continued down this same course of action with almost anyone who would dare to disagree with me. Amber was just one of the many casualties of my self-righteousness and judgmental behavior.

As time continued, however, this just didn't seem right. After a period of time, I decided to examine my actions. Even though I was very young, I started to question if I was doing Christianity correctly. It was as if something was missing.

As dedicated as I was, I just felt like I was going through the motions. I started questioning some of my beliefs. It was nothing major. I never questioned my beliefs about God, the Bible, Jesus, or moral living. I did question some of the beliefs that my specific church affiliation taught, however.

Some of the things I was being told just didn't seem to make sense. One time at church when I questioned a belief, I was instructed to study more. I was told in another instance that I was too young to comprehend the arguments and I would understand as I got older.

When I got a little older, I still didn't understand many of the distinguishing beliefs that were taught at my church. Don't get me wrong, I understood what they were and I understood why we believed them. I could quote them better than anyone in my class. I just wasn't convinced of some of the argumentation.

Instead of studying and coming to my own conclusions, I was expected to have the exact same beliefs as everyone else at my church even if I was "too young to understand or comprehend it." That just didn't sound like faith to me. For a very brief period of time, I decided to reject some of the positions of my church affiliation.

I want to reiterate. I didn't reject Christianity. Rather, I rejected some of our church rituals and traditions, especially as it pertained to how we condemned others who didn't have *all* the *exact* same rituals, answers, beliefs, and traditions as we did.

During this short span, I began to live a more grace-centered style of Christianity. I was finding freedom in places I hadn't before and becoming friends with other believers I once would have condemned.

Even though I was just a teenager, members at my church were voicing their concern for me. Some viewed me as questioning truth and they were fearful I was leaving what they deemed as the "one faith" (Eph. 4:5; Jude 3).

This seemed very odd to me. I didn't understand why they were concerned. I believed in God. I believed the Bible. I believed in the death, burial, and resurrection of Jesus Christ. I trusted in Jesus and I was living a much purer moral life than most of their children. Why were they so concerned about me?

The things I questioned didn't have to do so much with Christianity as it did with church tradition. It didn't seem like a big deal to me. However, members at my church thought it was a big deal. Many were worried I was going in the direction of error. However, their worries would soon be over.

CHAPTER 10
A NEW FRIENDSHIP

It can be hard to question your beliefs at any age, but especially when you're a teenager. In reality, your beliefs are still forming which makes it a very tricky time.

While I was questioning some of the particular beliefs within my church affiliation, I became good friends with a guy named "Jason." Jason was a preacher's kid. His dad wasn't the preacher at our specific congregation, but we were all part of the same church affiliation.

They lived close enough to us that he and I became great friends and we started to hang out all the time. We were the same age and had a lot in common. My friend's dad, "Mr. Williams," seemed to have a Bible answer for everything and not just an answer, but a Bible verse to go with it. I had never heard a better preacher than Mr. Williams.

Throughout the course of my friendship with Jason, his father became aware I had been questioning some beliefs within our church affiliation. I had high respect for Mr. Williams and was willing to listen to what he said. He approached me one night while I was staying the night with Jason and he asked if he could talk to me about some of my questions.

Mr. Williams said he promised to tell me only what the Bible had to say and he would never give me his opinion, but only truth from the Bible. This sounded great! From the perspective of a teenager, his knowledge seemed infinite. Therefore, I began to bring him my concerns and questions.

For every question I had, Mr. Williams provided an answer. I could tell he had heard these questions before. He told me I should never have questioned in the first place because "we" already have the truth. From that point forward, I was hooked. I wanted to be mentored by Mr. Williams because I saw the zeal he had for God. It was contagious. I wanted that same zeal.

He was fearless and wasn't afraid to talk to anyone about the Bible. When he preached, he would even call out specific names of those he believed were false teachers. He didn't care whose feelings he hurt because he believed he was preaching the truth. I wanted to be just like him.

I went to Jason's house often to spend the night, but instead of hanging out with Jason, I would end up studying Greek and Hebrew with Mr. Williams. I craved knowledge. The more I learned about the Bible, the more I wanted to learn about the Bible.

Similar to Adam and Eve, the knowledge of good and evil became my obsession (1 Cor. 8:1). Mr. Williams and I started a Bible website together. He made me feel elite. I was one of the few "faithful" Christians.

Our website predominantly focused on "refuting" the "false" beliefs of other churches that didn't do everything the way we did them. The focus was on what we were doing correctly and what other church affiliations were doing wrong. We would even condemn others within our church affiliation who didn't believe everything just like us.

He taught me how to write articles and I started writing quite a few in my teenage years that were published by a couple of organizations. Eventually, I found myself closer to Mr. Williams than I did to Jason. We just had more in common.

When I was 17 years old, he asked if I would like to preach at his church one Sunday evening. He told me he would help me prepare a lesson. I agreed and ended up preaching about the subject of death. The sermon title was, "What If You Die Tonight?", and I talked about my sister dying and how we should always be ready to meet God. After I finished, I knew I wanted to be a preacher. When there was an opportunity, Mr. Williams continued to let me speak occasionally at his church.

Later on, he told me there was a church looking for a part-time preacher and that he could connect me with them. I was very excited about this opportunity and decided I would try out for the position. They were a small church of around 30 people at the time. They needed someone to come on Sundays to preach while their other preacher was away for a while.

After I tried out, they offered me the job. I was more than willing to accept the challenge to start preaching on a regular basis. I was excited to see what the future would hold for me.

CHAPTER 11
OVER-INFLATED EGO

I greatly enjoyed my time preaching for that small country church. The church was filled with a group of excellent people. Of course, I now feel sorry for them since they had to endure the preaching of Kevin Pendergrass during his teenage years. Nevertheless, they did tolerate me and they were very encouraging.

The more I studied and preached, the more I knew that was what I wanted to do for the rest of my life. During this time, Mr. Williams continued to train me. I was soaking up everything he had to say like a sponge.

Even though I didn't realize it, in reality, he was my authority. If you disagreed with him, then you were wrong. I always sided with my mentor, Mr. Williams. I really idolized him.

Mr. Williams did everything he could to help me find extra speaking engagements. Since a teenage preacher is somewhat of a novelty, I began to receive invitations to speak at events such as camps, retreats, and youth rallies. I received way more praise than was necessary or what was deserved.

Unfortunately, I began to believe my own "newspaper clippings." The rare time someone would say something negative or give me some helpful criticism, I would ignore it and brush it off as someone wanting to change me.

Mr. Williams would tell me those are just people wanting to water down my preaching. He told me that they were jealous because they didn't have "my boldness." I naturally started to compare myself to other speakers and noticed that I was blunter and harsher in my presentation. While I was simply mimicking Mr. William's style of preaching, I personally enjoyed it as well. It distinguished us from other preachers.

I asked Mr. Williams why we were different from other preachers. He told me that not all preachers in our church affiliation are actually upholding the truth. He warned me not to be like them. He told me there were a lot of preachers compromising and sugarcoating the truth.

He told me that I was going to be one of the preachers who could restore things in our church affiliation to the way they needed to be if I dedicated myself to the cause.

Between Mr. Williams inflating my already oversized ego and all the constant compliments I received at various speaking engagements, I started to believe my own hype. I had convinced myself that I was the second-best preacher. Mr. Williams was the "absolute best," of course.

I started to take some Bible classes at a school in Nashville, Tennessee. Mr. Williams told me it would be good if I went on to higher education. However, he warned me about the dangers of attending Christian universities. He said most Christian universities aren't even worth attending since there are so many "false teachers" at those schools. I asked him what he suggested.

He said that instead of attending a Christian college, I should attend a school of preaching. Some know these as seminaries. A school of preaching or seminary focuses predominantly on the Bible and Bible-related issues.

He told me that a preaching school would train me much better than a Christian university. I remember him jokingly telling me it was like a Bible boot camp.

He said instead of taking a couple of classes a day, I would be in class all day long. Therefore, with Mr. William's advice and encouragement, I decided to take the next step to higher education. This is when I began to take on my own identity.

PART 4:
LIFE IN PREACHING SCHOOL

CHAPTER 12
A NEW JOURNEY BEGINS

I moved to Tennessee in 2006 to begin my studies in preaching school. Even though I was the youngest at the school during this time, I had more experience preaching than most of the other students. To put it politely, I was very arrogant. Of course, I just called it confidence. I thought I already had all of the major answers and school was just there to give me my credentials.

I found that Mr. Williams was right about the heavy workload of a preaching school. Our classes typically lasted from 8:00 a.m. until 4:30 p.m. In order to attend this specific school, you had to agree to not work outside of your classes because the academic workload was so great. Going to this school was literally a full-time job.

Since we couldn't work, students were financially supported by churches and individuals within our religious affiliation. During the course of the two-year program, we covered every single verse of every book in the Bible.

We also had classes on church history, world religions, the Greek and Hebrew languages, and a host of other topics. Because the intensity level was so high, a student in our class dropped out after the first year.

Preaching school would prove to be a very interesting time in my life. It didn't take me very long to begin debating with my professors and other students. I was becoming a very argumentative person.

If there was any biblical point of disagreement (no matter how large or small), I would raise my hand and explain why I thought my professors and fellow students were wrong. I wasn't just going to accept what they said. Unfortunately, I had much more confidence and zeal than I did common sense and knowledge.

During this time, I started to pick up on some of the same subtle inconsistencies within our church affiliation that once bothered me as a young teenager.

For example, one professor would hold a different view on a Bible subject than another professor. Yet, both professors would teach that in order to have unity, we must agree with one another. I began to notice that everyone was not on the same page and in agreement like I had thought.

Just because they were inconsistent didn't mean I had to be inconsistent, though. Therefore, I would point out these inconsistencies to my professors. This ended up leading to many one-on-one meetings with my professors after class.

I even remember reporting one of my professors, "Mr. Parker," to one of the leaders of the school for teaching "false doctrine." One of the leaders, "Mr. Foster," told me that while he may disagree with Mr. Parker, we all must learn to live together in unity.

I told Mr. Foster if he was going to disregard the truth in such a manner, we might as well just fellowship and accept anyone and everyone. He told me there are some issues that matter and some that don't matter to our salvation. I told him I agreed, but I asked him how he was gauging the difference. He never provided the answer for me.

As far as I was concerned, either you were right or you were wrong. If someone was wrong, they needed to change their belief. In my mind, it was that simple and I was willing to do whatever it took to be consistent with my beliefs. With this mentality, I would soon do something on a major scale that would impact me and the school as a whole.

CHAPTER 13
WALK THE WALK

While at school, we had multiple classes in which we were taught the importance of refuting false doctrine. We were instructed that correction needed to take place if someone was teaching false doctrine. We were told that if someone was publicly teaching false doctrine, then it needed to be corrected publicly. I was willing to put this teaching to the test.

While at preaching school, we went to several different seminars and lectureships. The largest lectureship we attended is associated with a Christian university. During this lectureship, there is a daily session called "Open Forum." It is the largest attended session with around 3,000 people in attendance.

Open Forum is a time where one of the professors from the university discusses Bible-related issues and questions submitted by members of the audience.

During this time, the professor gives his take on the subject and when he is finished, anyone can go up to the microphone to ask questions or make comments. This particular day, the professor, "Dr. West," voiced his opinion about a subject. I completely disagreed with his belief.

The subject he discussed that day had been a controversial topic within our church affiliation. It had to do with a long-held tradition in worship.

Many in the audience opposed Dr. West's conclusion and even some within leadership positions at the preaching school where I attended opposed the conclusion of Dr. West. In fact, the belief that

Dr. West was espousing about worship had been discussed at our school and had been deemed as "false doctrine."

After Dr. West was finished, he invited anyone to come to the microphone for their thoughts. I rushed up to the microphone in front of everyone. I told him he needed to repent because he was teaching false doctrine. Furthermore, I told him that the university needed to repent for allowing him to teach such "heresy."

You could hear a pin drop in the auditorium. After the session was over, Mr. Foster from school told me I was wrong for correcting Dr. West and I needed to apologize to him. This was very confusing to me.

I asked Mr. Foster if he believed that Dr. West was teaching false doctrine. He said he agreed Dr. West was teaching false doctrine. So, I asked Mr. Foster why I needed to apologize to him. If Dr. West was teaching false doctrine publicly and I corrected him publicly, then what did I do wrong?

Mr. Foster responded by telling me I should have handled it in a more gracious way. After listening to Mr. Foster, I was more than willing to agree with him in regards to how I handled the situation. I told him I was nervous and I admitted I could have said it better. However, either Dr. West was teaching false doctrine or he wasn't teaching false doctrine.

Later on, Mr. Foster called me into a private meeting to tell me that now he wasn't willing to say that Dr. West was teaching false doctrine. He told me that while he disagreed with Dr. West, he believed we could all agree to disagree on this issue.

As the weeks progressed, this began to turn into a big deal. Some churches who supported the preaching school believed the leadership should dismiss me from the school while other churches who supported the preaching school believed I did the right thing.

The preaching school's solution was for me to write a public apology in one of our church affiliate's publications. I told them I refused to do that. I wasn't sorry for what I did (at the time).

I believed I had the truth and that Dr. West was teaching false doctrine. I asked them how I could apologize for something about which I am not sorry.

I told them they could apologize on behalf of the school if they wanted to, but they couldn't apologize for my actions because I was convinced that I did the right thing.

While I received some opposition to what I did that day when I rebuked Dr. West, I received an overwhelmingly positive response by people throughout the whole United States within our church affiliation who had attended or heard about the incident.

I received e-mails, text messages, phone calls, and letters of encouragement. I made it known that day that no longer would "false teaching" be tolerated by "faithful men" like me.

I wanted people to know that I was going to lead a new generation of preachers into spiritual battle who weren't going to "play politics" or let false teachers get away with their false doctrine.

This experience made me even more adamant about making sure I was being consistent with my beliefs. When it came to applying what I had been taught, I was willing to do whatever it took, regardless of the consequences.

This whole situation would put a damper on my relationship with Mr. Foster and other professors at my school. I refused to go the "political" route. Instead of giving in to the pressure, I decided to stand my ground when it came to my convictions. This would make the remainder of my time at preaching school even more difficult than it was already.

CHAPTER 14
STANDING MY GROUND

After the events from the last chapter occurred, things got a bit awkward at school to say the least. In addition to my other schoolwork, Mr. Foster required me to write an extra paper defending my actions against Dr. West. When I turned the paper in, Mr. Foster said it wasn't good enough and told me that I needed to rewrite it.

At this point, I knew things were not going to be easy for me. I seriously thought about transferring schools. In fact, I had a director at another preaching school reach out to me to see if I wanted to transfer and come to their school.

While I was tempted to do so, Mr. Williams, my mentor, told me I needed to stay where I was and commit to doing my best. Besides, there were many other professors at the preaching school who supported me. In reality, I had more support from my school than I realized, but the opposition just seemed overwhelming at the time.

In fact, several years after I graduated, another professor at the preaching school told me he had disagreed with how the school handled the situation with me and, during that time, some of the leadership was hoping I would leave school. He told me that he was glad I decided to stay there.

As time passed during preaching school, I became even more dogmatic about my views and positions because I saw the inconsistency in others and I didn't want to be that way.

oticed how some preachers would call something a sin, but they wouldn't follow through with the teaching in practice. Or they would only act on it if they had enough support from their colleagues. I vowed not to be like them. I was going to be different. I was going to follow through and be consistent with my beliefs.

I became a product of the very system I was taught. Everywhere I turned, division seemed inevitable. Every time someone brought up a topic or had a belief I didn't agree with, I felt obligated to "correct" them.

Looking back, it is now clear to me that I really viewed my cause as one of correcting those I deemed to be false teachers. My Christianity was about confirming how "right" I was and correcting all of those who were "wrong."

In my final year of preaching school, I had a professor who seemed to be a lot like my mentor, Mr. Williams. His name was "Mr. Collins." Mr. Collins personally told me he agreed with how I handled Dr. West and asked if I would like to have an internship to work alongside him.

He told me it wouldn't be a job, but I would be able to attend his church and do some part-time preaching and teaching. I gladly accepted and began my internship with Mr. Collins.

CHAPTER 15
SAME SONG, DIFFERENT VERSE

I was very excited to be working with Mr. Collins. He was down to earth, a very hard worker, and really seemed to care for people. As the weeks turned into months, Mr. Collins and I became much closer.

He started to confide in me about certain things at the church. He specifically told me about one man there, "Mr. Ross," who, according to Mr. Collins, was a troublemaker.

Mr. Ross was one of the leaders at the church there, but getting along with him was difficult. Based upon what Mr. Collins told me, I decided to keep my eye on Mr. Ross. Inevitably, a topic came up about which Mr. Ross and I disagreed. In my typical fashion, I tried to correct him.

Mr. Ross wasn't going to take anything from a young man like myself. He told me there was nothing I could do and that he "ran" that church. I would soon prove him wrong.

The following Sunday, I was scheduled to lead the opening prayer. With Mr. Ross and his family in attendance, I specifically prayed that Mr. Ross would come forward and repent of his "sins." You could hear people gasping from their pews.

After the service, Mr. Ross came up to me. Naturally, he was fuming from what I had said earlier in the service. Several of us met and I was told by the leadership that I could no longer work as an intern at that church.

I was left feeling very discouraged. It was difficult on Mr. Collins as well. He and I still kept in touch, but I was no longer able to work alongside him. I felt as if my life was on constant repeat. I was following through with what I was being taught and then punished for it. However, this didn't stop me from continuing to do what I believed was right.

My attempted consistency didn't go unnoticed by others. Five months before I graduated, I was offered an opportunity to be part of one of the largest ministries in my church affiliation. It was a multimedia ministry based in Oklahoma that consisted of TV and radio programs that were aired worldwide.

They were familiar with the way I had handled Dr. West and told me they applauded my actions and were looking for "faithful men" like me. They ended up flying me out to Oklahoma to try out for the position. From the moment I arrived, I hit it off with everyone who worked at that ministry. While I was there, I was offered the job and gladly accepted.

By the time I graduated from preaching school in 2008, I thought that I knew everything there was to know about the Bible and I was now fully ready to begin my ministry in Oklahoma.

Before we move on to my days in Oklahoma, I want to emphasize there are so many more stories, like the ones I have shared, that I could tell you about that happened while I was in preaching school.

However, if I could sum it up, I would say that I was an immature, overly zealous Christian who used little to no tact, but who truly believed I was doing the right thing and was trying to be consistent with my belief system (even if those around me were not).

I was willing to do whatever my convictions led me to do, regardless of the consequences. When I moved to Oklahoma to begin my ministry, things would get much worse before they would get better.

PART 5: MINISTRY OF MASS DESTRUCTION

CHAPTER 16
MY CAREER TAKES OFF

Oklahoma is where I found my fresh start out of preaching school in my early twenties. I thought I had it made working with one of the largest ministries in my church affiliation.

I was originally hired to be the marketer and fundraiser of the program. My job was to go to as many churches as I possibly could in order to educate them about our ministry and raise financial support for our program.

The program was a TV and radio ministry that provided free Bible materials to churches and individuals. I really liked the idea of offering everything for free. Whereas many religious programs always seem to be trying to get their viewers to send money, we made it a point to never ask for money on our show.

After working there for a couple of weeks, I was offered the opportunity to speak for several of the TV episodes on a trial basis. This was something I hoped would happen one day, but I didn't expect to have the chance so soon.

The trial basis went very well and I became the co-host of the TV and radio programs within the first few months of my move to Oklahoma.

I loved the flexibility of my job. A standard workweek included recording lessons for TV and radio and then traveling to different churches throughout the week. I became a figurehead for the program. I would usually travel on Wednesday nights and the weekends to speak since this is when most churches hold their meetings and assemblies. It wasn't rare for me to travel to three churches per week.

While working with the program, I personally spoke at over 200 churches. Some of those churches were smaller in number (under thirty members) and some of them were larger in number (over one thousand members).

I traveled to many locations during my stint with the program. This included churches in Oklahoma, Texas, Alabama, Tennessee, Missouri, Kansas, Connecticut, Virginia, West Virginia, North Carolina, Florida, Kentucky, Georgia, Indiana, Michigan, and Wisconsin. Needless to say, I felt like I was big stuff.

Aside from the specific churches where I actually preached, I was in contact with over 500 churches. Since I wasn't always able to visit every church that supported us, I would make phone calls on a daily basis to inform our supporters about updates within our ministry.

Working with such a large number of congregations afforded me the opportunity to meet a wide range of people from different areas and backgrounds.

I felt very blessed to be able to get out among so many different people. While most preachers are only able to work among their own congregation, I was able to work among hundreds of congregations.

I started to gain the reputation of being fearless in my preaching. I had many churches tell me that I was willing to speak on topics and subjects that other preachers were too afraid to address publicly. Therefore, churches began to invite me to come out specifically to address certain controversial topics or situations they were dealing with at their church at the time.

People began to come to me for answers. I liked that. I liked it a lot. I felt like I had a "Bible answer" for everything. If someone else didn't know it, I would be sure to let you know that I knew it. I allowed this kind of exposure to go to my head and continue to inflate my ego. I fed on this idea and it became my identity. I liked the idea of being the fearless and bold preacher. It was as if I were bulletproof.

As such, many of my sermons purposely centered around controversial topics with my explanation always being "correct." Since I assumed that I was correct and couldn't be wrong, those who disagreed with me were wrong and couldn't be correct.

Not only were they "wrong," but they needed to change to see things just like I saw them. Looking back, this arrogance caused me to have a distorted view of others. I'll explain this in the next chapter.

CHAPTER 17
DISTORTED VIEW OF OTHERS

I used to begin all of my conversations with the presupposition that I was right and would not even entertain the thought I could be wrong. You might be thinking that infallibility was a pretty impressive feat for someone to have accomplished in their twenties. I would never have told you I thought I was infallible, but my beliefs and actions proved otherwise.

I had bought into a false presupposition without realizing it. A presupposition is when you enter into a conversation or study already believing something to be true. Presuppositions are not bad in and of themselves. We all have presuppositions. In fact, they are essential.

Presuppositions only become a problem when we are not mindful or honest about them. One of my presuppositions was very dangerous because I had tricked myself into believing I couldn't be wrong on biblical matters.

Theoretically, I would have changed if I could have been proven wrong. But in application, I didn't allow for the possibility of being wrong, at least not on any matters I thought were of any significance.

In Bible conversations with others, I always viewed myself as the teacher, not the student. I was the corrector who was constantly looking to correct others. If someone said something I even remotely disagreed with, I would immediately label it as false doctrine.

In my mind, I had the truth and those that dared oppose me did not have the truth. I couldn't be wrong and they couldn't be right. This false belief naturally impacted how I viewed others. I believed that if someone disagreed with me on biblical matters, the reason he or she disagreed boiled down to one of two things:

1. He/she is ignorant and has not been properly taught and just needs to keep studying the Bible.

2. He/she is dishonest and is purposefully refusing to do the right thing.

Since I was one of the "few, faithful" Christians, this meant I thought almost everyone I came in contact with was either ignorant or dishonest.

If I perceived someone as ignorant about a biblical subject, I would try to have as many Bible studies with them as possible to teach them what I believed to be the truth.

If I perceived them as dishonest, I condemned them as a heretic, labeled them a false teacher, and would "mark" them (Rom. 16:17). In my mind, those who disagreed with me were the divisive ones.

I would always have a reason why they should be discredited if someone failed to agree with me after I taught them what I believed to be the truth. After all, in my mind, if they really wanted to follow God, they would be doing what I told them.

If they rejected what I said, there had to be a specific reason. I never considered the possibility that I could be wrong. In reality, I was no different than the Jews who always tried to discredit Jesus and His followers.[11]

I would make accusations against those who disagreed with me such as: "They are out to destroy truth;" "They are only interested in making a big name for themselves;" "They just want money;" "They

---

[11] Acts 26:24; Mt. 13:55; Jn. 1:46; Lk. 4:24

want power and control;" "They are cowards;" "They aren't willing to be persecuted for Jesus;" and "They aren't truly dedicated to Christ."

The list of accusations goes on and on without end. When it came to those with whom I disagreed, I always found myself judging their intent. The above accusations could be multiplied but should be sufficient to make the point that when you are looking for reasons to discredit someone, then one reason is just as good as another.

It wasn't that I was purposely making up an ulterior motive for the person, it was just that I had to have some reason to rationalize to myself why someone wouldn't obey what I believed to be the truth. There had to be some explanation. Therefore, I was more than willing to supply possibilities that would help explain the reason.

Furthermore, when I convinced myself that the other person really didn't care about God, then I didn't have to listen to them.

This mentality really did distort my view of the human race. From my perspective at the time, I was a righteous Christian who constantly happened to find myself surrounded by a bunch of ignorant and dishonest sinners. This attitude was predicated on the fact that I believed I was always right.

I had an extremely high view of myself and a very low view of anyone who disagreed with me. This made it easy for me to be very mean toward others without realizing I was being mean. Besides, I used the Bible to justify how I would treat and talk to others who disagreed with me. After all, Jesus turned the tables, didn't He?

CHAPTER 18
TURNING THE TABLES

While I had quite a few people who appreciated my blunt and straightforward style, others believed that I was lacking proper love. They told me they agreed with what I did, but not how I did it. In other words, they thought my belief was correct, just not my approach.

I could not stand this accusation and I was willing to "correct" anyone who would dare try to accuse me of not "loving souls." I remember one night when I was the visiting preacher for a church, one man told me that he agreed 100 percent with what I said, but he disagreed 100 percent with how I said it. I told him I believe we are to speak the truth in love (Eph. 4:15). I told him that I speak the truth because I love souls.

I asked this man if Elijah was loving when he mocked the prophets of Baal (1 Kgs. 18:20-40). Was Paul being kind when, with an intent look on his face, he rebuked Elymas and identified him as a "son of the devil" (Acts 13:9)? Oh, trust me, I had my "rebuttals" ready. When I called someone's name publicly to condemn them, I would reference how Jesus did the same thing (Mt. 23). When people would walk out of my sermons because I made them mad, I would remind the rest of the audience how Jesus constantly offended and "ran people away" (Jn. 6:60-66).[12]

When I would "name-call," I pointed out that John sharply rebuked the Jews for being a "brood of vipers" and commanded them to repent of their sins (Lk. 3:7-18). This list is only the tip of

---

[12]Mt. 13:57; Mk. 6:3; Mt. 15:12; 11:6; Mk. 10:17-22

the iceberg when it came to verses that I used to "justify" my actions and my tact (or lack thereof). Of course, my favorite examples that I used was when Jesus scared away the moneychangers twice, turning their tables over with a whip of cords in His hand (Jn. 2:13-22; Mt. 21:12-17).

When I would quote these passages to defend my actions, no one could refute them. I knew I was right and I was going to prove it! Instead of people changing, they typically became upset at me. When that happened, I used the words of Paul when he said, "Have I now become your enemy by telling you the truth" (Gal. 4:16)? I made countless "enemies" during this time. It was similar to the snowball effect. My approach became relentless. In the next few chapters, I will give some specific examples.

CHAPTER 19
TAKE IT OUTSIDE

In traveling to a host of different churches, I had the luxury of being the guest preacher. So, I thought nothing of the damage oftentimes left behind in my wake. In my mind, I knew all the answers to any Bible questions you could ask me. I didn't have just one Bible verse to answer your question; I had at least two or three.

For example, one time I traveled to West Virginia to preach. It was the first time I had ever been to this particular congregation and didn't personally know anyone there. Everyone was very kind to me and they treated me very well.

We had several visitors who came every night of the meeting. On Tuesday night, we had a husband and wife couple who visited the church. During my sermon, I could tell they were visibly upset at some of the things I said. About 15 minutes into the lesson, they ended up walking out of the church building.

Instead of continuing to preach, I paused my sermon. I told the church I would be right back. I left the building and followed this couple out into the parking lot. I told them they were disrespectful for walking out of my lesson and that they needed to repent of their actions.

This turned into a heated exchange. The couple kept trying to get in their car and leave, but I continued to pursue them. Finally, when they got away from me, I went back into the church building and finished my sermon.

Episodes like this occurred practically everywhere I went. I would stir up drama without realizing I was the cause. I always blamed the problems on everyone else.

On another occasion, I angered a man so much that he almost punched me at a church in Oklahoma where I was a guest speaker. I had called him out during my lesson and after the sermon was over, he met me in the parking lot and started to shove me and tell me he was going to put me in my place. Thankfully, there were others around who got between us.

When I was a guest speaker at a church in Arkansas, I ran a few visitors away and made them mad because I made the statement that, "If you don't want to be at church right now, then we don't want you to be here, either."

Every time someone would get mad at me, I would claim I was the victim and the "martyr" for Jesus because I was being "persecuted" for doing the "right" thing.

I would quote passages about persecution and say things such as, "Well, the Bible teaches we will be persecuted when we uphold the truth."[13]

Instead of instances like these causing me to second guess things, I believed that this was further proof and affirmation I was doing the right thing. Aside from my travels to speak at different churches, I also didn't mind being blunt in my formal debates. I'll discuss that in the next chapter.

---

[13] 2 Tim. 3:12; 1 Pet. 4:12-14; Jn. 15:18; 1 Jn. 3:13; etc.

CHAPTER 20
DISRESPECT

During this time, I had a great interest in public debating. It seemed to be a lost art and not too many preachers were debating anymore. Therefore, I wanted to try and bring back more public debating within Christianity.

I was one of the youngest formal debaters in my church affiliation. Mr. Williams, my mentor, always trained and prepared me for my debates. Even though we didn't get to see each other very often, we kept in touch almost on a daily basis through phone calls and e-mail.

My first public debate was in 2009. The man I debated was 78 years old. Instead of stating my beliefs respectfully, I put on quite a spectacle. I screamed, yelled, condemned the man, told him how ignorant he was, mocked him, and I was the self-proclaimed winner of the debate.

After my first debate, I enjoyed it so much that I immediately started to try and schedule more debates.

I even flew to Canada to debate Mr. George Ramocan who, at the time, was a diplomat and had been a senator for Jamaica. Just as I did with my other debates, I went right after him and didn't just address his arguments, but I also attacked him personally.

When it came to *anyone* who disagreed with me, I would treat them with absolutely no respect. I was very rude. Of course, at the time, I didn't view my actions as rude or disrespectful. I only thought I was contending for the faith and doing the right thing (Jude 3).

Some have asked me how I could have justified my behavior during this time. The answer is I had convinced myself that I was doing the right thing (see Chapter 18). To me, what I was doing *was* Christianity.

In fact, I would ask others during this time why they weren't out doing what I was doing in the way I was doing it. Even if people believed the same things I did, it was not enough. They had to be as aggressive and blunt as I was about it. Otherwise, I would accuse them of being weak, a sissy, and watered down.

The last debate I had in 2013 was probably my "worst" debate in terms of how I handled myself. It basically turned into a screaming match. Because of how I acted, even some who agreed with my proposition couldn't bring themselves to watch the debate. At the same time, I also had quite a bit of support.

People either loved me or hated me. I say hate quite deliberately. There wasn't much middle ground. The people who didn't like my style really didn't like my style and the people who did like my style couldn't get enough of it.

Whenever I would meet someone who was like me, I would make sure to stay in contact with them so we could keep one another encouraged to keep "fighting the good fight."

CHAPTER 21
CHURCH CRASHERS

Aside from debating and causing all kinds of drama when I would go to churches to preach, my friends and I also wreaked havoc on other churches, too.

It wasn't rare for my buddies and me to go to another church and interrupt their service to tell them what they were doing wrong.

Brandon Johnson, my best friend who wrote the foreword to this book, and I went to a church service where they publicly advertised that they were going to heal anyone who wanted to be healed of any infirmities.

Instead of us going and kindly discussing our disagreements with them, we decided to do things a bit differently. These individuals claimed they could raise the dead, drink poison, and not be affected, etc. So, we thought we would go and test the waters (1 Jn. 4:1).

During the service, they said if anyone wanted a miracle, all you had to do was come forward and they would heal you. Brandon went forward and told them his eyesight was bad and he didn't want to have to wear glasses anymore. They told him that they could heal him. By the way, I recorded this whole event as it took place.

Needless to say, Brandon still wears glasses. In front of everyone, we told them they were false teachers. While everyone was watching, I told them that if we were to go to the graveyard right now and they told the dead to rise and I told them to stay down, we would win.

We also challenged them to drink poison to prove to everyone they could actually drink poison and not be harmed (Of course, we would never have actually allowed them to do it). They refused to do it and said we didn't have enough faith. But they said they had enough faith when I asked them. Therefore, I told them we would drink poison and they could heal us.

They didn't take us up on that offer, either. We eventually got kicked out of that church and were told to never come back. We were actually kicked out of several churches for interrupting and disrupting their services.

As proof of how righteous we were and how unfaithful everyone else was, we would sometimes record these events to show others. At other times, we would just go into churches and catch their preacher off guard with a few questions.

If they couldn't answer them automatically, we would "bully" them and tell them they didn't have the truth. From our perspective, we were not being bullies; we were just "rebuking" them and "contending for the faith" (Jude 3).

Several churches threatened to call the cops before they could get us to leave and one friend of mine actually was arrested for not leaving the premises at a church one time.

Another friend of mine and I would go door knocking and as soon as the resident answered, we would ask them if they were part of our church affiliation. If they weren't, we told them if they didn't change then they were going to go to hell.

On one occasion, a preacher drove to where I lived and confronted me because I had previously called him out in front of other people. I ended up "rebuking" him for three hours and he almost had to go to the hospital because of his blood pressure.

When he tried to leave, I continued to rebuke him. I told him if he was going to drive all this way to talk to me, he was also going to hear what I had to say to him.

Besides all of this, I also participated in the typical Facebook banter and other useless social media discussions. I would call people by name on social media to "mark" them as false teachers or call out their sin publicly to shame them so they would repent of their "sins."

While many other things could be said, this is just a small snapshot of my life in ministry at that point. Once again, I want to reiterate that I was very sincere during this time. I *thought* I was doing the right thing in the right way. I had no ill intent.

During this time, I was gaining a following. As time went on, I was promoted to director of the ministry. I had gone from being the marketer and fundraiser to co-host to now director of the whole ministry and I was only in my mid-twenties.

Needless to say, I was very proud of my resume and didn't mind touting it to others. By beginning my preaching career at the age of 17, co-hosting international TV and radio programs, becoming one of the youngest formal debaters in my church affiliation in my early twenties, and directing one of the largest ministries within our affiliation by the age of 25, I felt bulletproof.

PART 6:
A DANGEROUS MENTALITY

CHAPTER 22
CONFIRMATION BIAS

It is now clear how closed-minded I was looking back on that portion of my life. The irony in this is that I was the one always accusing others of being closed-minded. I had tricked myself into believing I was the open-minded person.

I had fallen prey to confirmation bias. Confirmation bias is when one searches for information in a way that will only confirm one's preexisting beliefs.[14] This cognitive bias is most pronounced in the case of ingrained, ideological, or emotionally charged views.

This is why so many Jews rejected Jesus when He came to earth. In their minds, they were looking for the Messiah to establish a physical kingdom and be their physical king like David.[15]

Instead of being corrected by Jesus, they allowed their ingrained ideological beliefs to blind them to the point of crucifying Jesus.[16]

It is for this reason that the most studied and knowledgeable leaders of the day missed it. As Jesus put it, they were the "blind leading the blind" (Mt. 15:14).

When I disagreed with someone, I didn't put much effort into understanding the real reasons. I didn't put the proper time into studying things from their perspective. I didn't really know their arguments and reasons for their belief. Don't get me wrong. I thought I knew their reasons. I was confident that I knew the

---

[14] www.dictionary.com/browse/confirmation-bias?s=t
[15] Mt. 3:2; Lk. 22:29; Mk. 9:1; Eph. 1:20-22; Acts 2:29-39; Col. 1:16-18
[16] 1 Cor. 2:6-10

"opponent's view" better than they knew it. This is very important to understand because you can think you know why someone believes something, but actually fail to understand the real reasons.

If we are not careful, we can get so entangled in the idea of thinking we can't be wrong that we easily misrepresent others. It is easy to take a sentence or a paragraph from something and misrepresent it instead of making sure we are fully understanding the point.

I used to shut people out immediately if I knew that someone didn't automatically conform to my way of thinking.

I would discredit positions simply because I had never heard of them. If it was a new idea, I wouldn't even entertain the possibility that I could be wrong. I assumed if a fine Bible student like myself had never heard a position or argument, then it must be wrong because if it was right, I would have already heard of it. I had a very arrogant attitude.

However, the truth of the matter is we are all guilty of confirmation bias to an extent. Let me demonstrate this point.

When we study something that we already disagree with, we usually approach it from the perspective of why it is wrong. When we study something that we already agree with, we usually approach it from the perspective of why it is right.

As humans, we are already at a subconscious disadvantage. From the outset, our minds are automatically approaching situations from a biased perspective.

This doesn't mean we should give up studying; it simply means we must admit that we all come to the table with biases and should strive to be as objective as possible.

This can only be done when we have "clothed ourselves with humility" (1 Pet. 5:5). Another way to put it is to say that humility is the best friend to objectiveness. On the other hand, the more arrogant someone is, the more they tend to be subjective and closed-minded.

Humility is vital in being open-minded and objective. Instead of being humble, I was very arrogant and thought I knew everything.

The road of pride leads to destruction and the road of humility leads to God (Prov. 16:18; Ja. 4:10). The arrogant are closed off to listening to others (Prov. 18:13; 15:22). Instead, they only wish to express their own heart and beliefs (Prov. 18:2; 28:26). It doesn't take any humility to admit we are right, but it does take humility to admit we are wrong.

When I first learned about confirmation bias, I was in a bit of denial that I could have ever fallen prey to it. After all, I was convinced that I was a logical and rational thinker and never biased in the way I approached a biblical subject.

Yet, I realized that, as humans, our pride makes it easy to believe we are always right. Immediate reassurance is much easier than in-depth research.

Unfortunately, those who are arrogant will never consider they are closed-minded because they are too proud to consider the fact they could be wrong. This is why the Bible says not to be wise in your own opinion (Prov. 3:7; Rom. 12:16).

Instead of clothing myself in humility, I had unknowingly immersed myself in arrogance. It was for this reason that I was the master at confirmation bias and didn't even have a clue.

CHAPTER 23
BELIEF PERSEVERANCE

Similar to confirmation bias is belief perseverance. Belief perseverance is slightly different. Confirmation bias has more to do with not even considering another point of view, whereas belief perseverance is how we respond when an alternative to our view is provided and we have to deal with our view being challenged.

Belief perseverance is the tendency to cling to one's initial belief even after receiving new information that contradicts or disconfirms the basis of that belief.[17]

Practically speaking, belief perseverance is when we are shown evidence to contradict a biased view, but we still interpret it in a manner that reinforces our current perspective.

After debating an issue, I would usually say something to the effect of, "Well, after talking with you, I am even more convinced I am right and you are wrong."

This is done in an attempt to convince ourselves we are right. If a good point has been made and we don't want to accept it, we will do everything we can to try and convince ourselves we are still right.

---

[17] Anderson, C.A. (2007). Belief perseverance (pp. 109-110). In R. F. Baumeister & K. D. Vohs (Eds.), Thousand Oaks, CA: Sage. Encyclopedia of Social Psychology.
https://public.psych.iastate.edu/caa/abstracts/2005-2009/07A.pdf

Warren Buffet is credited with saying, "What the human being is best at doing is interpreting all new information so that their prior conclusions remain intact."[18]

Belief perseverance can also happen when we choose to consider another viewpoint and perhaps even modify our current understanding, but only to the extent where it doesn't affect anything.

This is really the category in which I found myself. While I was certainly guilty of confirmation bias, I was even guiltier of belief perseverance. You see, I was never afraid to listen to another viewpoint. However, when I considered another viewpoint, it was always within a restricted framework.

When I read the writings of someone with whom I disagreed, I only read with the intent of proving them wrong instead of the purpose of actually learning or understanding the other person's perspective. I finally figured out there is a difference in studying the Bible and studying my own beliefs about the Bible. It can be very easy to confuse the two.

Just because someone knows their own beliefs very well doesn't mean they actually know the Bible. And just because someone knows what the Bible says doesn't mean they actually know what the Bible means (2 Tim. 2:15; Heb. 4:12). Remember, even Satan quoted Scripture (Mt. 4:1-11).

I was very dangerous because I knew what the Bible said. By age 26, I almost had the entire New Testament memorized by chapter. I also knew my belief system extremely well.

Since I was constantly engaging with others in debates and discussions, I was quick on my feet. For someone listening who is not a good Bible student, quoting a few verses and knowing your belief system can be very persuasive.

---

[18] www.quotefancy.com. Warren Buffet Quote

If you have ever been to an amusement park and ridden a water ride, you may have noticed that the water looks very deep. Yet, in reality, the water is very shallow.

If you were to get out of the boat, you would realize the water isn't deep at all. However, by remaining in the boat, it is easy to be convinced the water is very deep.

With my belief system, in a similar way, I made shallow waters look very deep by remaining in the boat. However, I didn't just convince others. I had convinced myself since I had never gotten out of the boat.

So, how does a closed-minded person change their mind? Better yet, how does a closed-minded person even realize they are being closed-minded? Naturally, closed-minded people will rarely consider they are closed-minded because they are closed-minded to the idea. Whew, that is a lot of closed-mindedness!

Telling a closed-minded person that they are closed-minded will only cause them to become more closed-minded. I had to realize for myself I was being closed-minded. This happened when I became invested enough in a situation and was personally affected to the point that it gave me a new perspective.

Jesus tells a parable about a son who took all of his inheritance, left his country, and quickly spent everything (Lk. 15:11-32). He then found himself destitute, in a pig sty, and at the point where he would have gladly eaten the pigs' slop.

Before this time, he had been too stubborn and closed-minded to consider alternatives to his situation. It wasn't until this humbling point in his life when it finally affected him enough for him to "come to himself" and realize the truth of the situation (Lk. 15:17).

In the same way, any closed-minded person must find themselves in a humbling situation where they will "come to themselves" and *honestly* consider a different perspective. I clearly remember the first time I realized I didn't have perfect understanding of biblical matters. I believe it was one of the moments that started the beginning of my spiritual change.

CHAPTER 24
A CHINK IN MY ARMOR

Whenever I preached, I emphasized I was only teaching truth from the Bible. I would explain the things I said were not my opinion, but the truth. I let it be known I had factual Bible answers for Bible questions.

From my perspective, any resistance to me was resistance to truth itself. To reject what I had to say was to reject what the Bible said. As far as I was concerned, what the Bible says and what I said were one and the same.

I had equated my beliefs with infallible truth. However, this began to slowly change when I realized that I actually could be wrong about biblical matters.

In 2010, when I was preparing for one of my formal debates, I was having difficulty with a Bible subject that, at the time, I believed really mattered. I was afraid because I started to question the consistency of a belief I had been taught and held all of my life.

I began to notice that the arguments I presented in my lessons in the past were not holding up to the scrutiny of Scripture in my in-depth debate preparation studies.

I realized that it was much easier to affirm a belief and preach it unchallenged to a group of people who already assumed I was right. A formal debate does not allow you that courtesy.

I read multiple books, articles, and debates hoping I could find something to justify my position. I "knew" I had truth. I just had to find the evidence. As each day came to an end, I became more anxious and afraid. In fact, few people know that I actually called the man I was going to debate to try and reschedule or cancel the debate. I didn't tell him why. I certainly didn't want to give my "opponent" any reason to believe I was questioning my own proposition.

Unfortunately, I had to press on and I wasn't able to get out of the debate. During this time, I reached out to my mentor, Mr. Williams, and several of my studious friends to pick their brains so they could help refute my silly doubt and I could go back to believing the "truth" on this particular subject.

Most of my friends just rehashed the same points I had already studied. Others told me they hadn't given the points I was bringing up much thought.

However, I briefly found some peace of mind when one friend, "Corey," told me that my questions had already been answered and refuted by preachers of the past and the arguments I had questions about were nothing new. I was relieved to hear this.

He told me to study and review the information he was going to send. When he sent the information to me, I was expecting to have my doubts washed away.

Instead, the more I studied the information, the more I realized the argumentation was very weak. I was hoping this information would answer my questions. It did not.

However, one friend, "Wes," responded differently. Just like all my close friends, I have great respect for him. He has a good understanding of Scripture. He is a very honest man and I have personally experienced his integrity.

To my surprise, he told me he had the same questions on the same issue and concluded he had been wrong and ended up changing his belief on the subject.

This was not the answer I was looking for because I was wanting someone to refute my doubt. He ended up giving me quite a bit of biblical information as to why he believed he had been wrong on this issue in the past and why he changed his mind on the matter.

As I read and studied the material, I couldn't help but realize that it made sense. I didn't like that it made sense because it was scary and uncomfortable. I didn't want it to make sense. So, what do you think I did in this situation?

Do you think I continued to explore my doubt? No. My mind retreated and my defenses were in full force. This is a prime example of not being objective.

I took the material he gave me to my other friends and told them we needed to refute this information. I did a quick turnaround to protect my peace of mind. In fact, I even began to try and discredit Wes. I told him he just needed to reconsider his belief and that he was on the wrong path.

He kindly asked me why I disagreed with his conclusion, especially seeing how I originally came to him to study the issue in the first place. Instead of addressing his question, I became defensive and told him that he wasn't going to play games with me and that he knew why he was wrong.

I even told him he should be ashamed of himself. However, later on I started looking more in depth at the material he gave me. It made sense, but what didn't make sense is how I could be wrong. I thought I already had the truth on this particular issue. How in the world could I have missed this?

My other friends didn't even care to read his material because in their minds they already "knew" he was wrong. They refused to consider his reasoning. I didn't want to consider it, but it was too late. After all, this was my original dilemma. I am the one that brought up all of this. I was invested in the situation and it affected me.

I remember asking myself a simple question: "Is it possible I could have been wrong on this issue for all of these years?" "No," I told myself. "No, there is no way. I know I am right." Yet, all the evidence pointed in the exact opposite direction. I continued to look for ways to refute his points.

I kept studying the Bible and many commentaries. I kept asking other preachers and friends for help. I researched and read article after article on the subject. Everything pointed to the fact that I could possibly be wrong.

Up until that point, I knew I had been wrong on matters I perceived to be small, but to me, this was a big matter and I had never been wrong on a big matter. Well, at least I had never contemplated the possibility I could be wrong. Needless to say, I eventually changed my understanding on that issue.

Looking back, I have come to believe that the particular subject I changed on isn't really that big of a deal. However, the effects of what happened in that instance were astronomical. It was the first time I can remember realizing I was wrong on a Bible subject that I thought was of significance. It was the first time I realized I had a chink in my armor.

PART 7:
RE-EXAMINING MY APPROACH TOWARD OTHERS

CHAPTER 25

AM I BEING CONSISTENT?

In Chapter 18, I covered how I justified my approach toward other people. I had an endless supply of Bible verses I could quote and allude to that, supposedly, justified my harsh treatment of others. As the months turned into years, however, I questioned if I was actually being consistent in my approach toward others.

I started to observe that when it came to my friends, I would "pull my punches" and not rebuke them as harshly. Had I blinded myself? The answer became very apparent when a situation arose with my mentor, Mr. Williams.

I had always respected Mr. Williams. He was the one man I could trust with my whole heart. We knew each other better than we knew ourselves. He had always been there for me and I had always been there for him.

However, an incident happened where I felt Mr. Williams was not practicing what he was preaching. I addressed him with this issue on several occasions and he told me that he agreed with me, but he was just waiting on the right time to do the right thing.

This answer pacified me because I didn't want to have to correct my own mentor. I certainly wasn't treating him like I had treated others who I thought were doing the wrong thing.

I noticed that I was playing favorites with my mentor. Finally, I decided to approach him about this situation once more. I told him he had been using time as an excuse and that he needed to do the right thing.

He continued to give excuse after excuse as I turned a blind eye to him and overlooked his situation in the name of mercy and grace because he was my mentor. I respected Mr. Williams and loved him more at that time than any other friend.

I finally admitted to myself that I had handled my friends and family completely differently when it came to biblical matters. If I disagreed with a friend or close family member, I would treat them with much more respect in my conversations than with those I didn't care for or didn't know as well.

Even the times I had to correct my friends or the times they had to correct me, the situation was still handled much differently. Much more prayer, tact, thought, and planning went into these situations.

I would give them grace and mercy while being extremely patient. On the other hand, if I didn't know someone well or if I didn't have a good relationship with them, I wouldn't think twice about acting brash and harsh toward them when dealing with biblical subjects.

Even when trying to justify my brash approach to people, I found myself being a hypocrite and showing favoritism (1 Tim. 5:21). This inadvertently showed me that I did believe it mattered how I said something. Otherwise, why was I handling the people I loved and cared about differently?

The reason is because deep down I do believe it matters how I handle people and I need to be careful with how I approach people and situations.

I had used all of the Bible verses previously discussed in Chapter 18 to justify my actions. However, what I came to realize was that these men in the Bible did not approach everyone the same way, nor did they handle every situation identically.

Yet, I found myself using these examples to aggressively and harshly rebuke anyone that I wanted to whenever I wanted to regardless of their intent, knowledge, offense, or situation.

The truth of the matter is that different people and situations will need to be handled accordingly. For example, in Acts 18:24-26, Aquila and Priscilla took Apollos aside and explained to him more accurately the Scriptures. They didn't condemn him. They didn't call him names. They didn't publicly humiliate or harass him.

I saw that instead of using wisdom and gentleness, I was using a one-size-fits-all approach. I was guilty of taking a handful of passages, isolating those passages, and then justifying my actions in light of those passages.

While some situations will warrant a harsh rebuke at times, this isn't always the case (Titus 1:13; Prov. 27:5; Psa. 141:5). In fact, I would argue that it usually isn't the case.

When harsh rebukes were given against sin, it was usually to the religious elite who were self-righteous (Mt. 23), leaders in the church who were held to a higher standard (Gal. 2:11; Heb. 13:17), or those who condoned and/or continued in blatant and rebellious sin (1 Cor. 5:1-2).

Furthermore, when the prophets of old or apostles would act aggressively, it was toward those who either vehemently opposed God/Jesus or those who were willfully sinning and didn't care about doing the right thing.

Not only had I dismissed the context of the passages that I used to allegedly justify my actions, but I had ignored the plain Bible verses that teach the importance of gentleness, tact, wisdom, and mercy. Consider the following verses:

> A gentle answer turns away wrath, but a harsh word stirs up anger. (Prov. 15:1).

Through patience a ruler can be persuaded, and a gentle tongue can break a bone. (Prov. 25:15).

Let your conversation be always full of grace, seasoned with salt, so that you may know how to answer everyone. (Col. 4:6).

Brothers and sisters, if someone is caught in a sin, you who live by the Spirit should restore that person gently. But watch yourselves, or you also may be tempted. Carry each other's burdens, and in this way you will fulfill the law of Christ. (Gal. 6:1-2).

And the Lord's servant must not be quarrelsome but must be kind to everyone, able to teach, not resentful. Opponents must be gently instructed, in the hope that God will grant them repentance leading them to a knowledge of the truth, and that they will come to their senses and escape from the trap of the devil, who has taken them captive to do his will. (2 Tim. 2:24-26).

When I began to read and study these passages, I slowly began to change my approach toward people. I didn't want to be inconsistent. I realized I needed to show mercy, grace, and patience to everyone, not just to those who were closest to me.

CHAPTER 26
CHECKING MY MOTIVATION

After seeing my own inconsistency in how I had been approaching other people, I was determined to show more grace and mercy in my approach toward others. The deeper I studied this topic, the more I saw that I had been a "jerk for Jesus" without realizing it.

Here I was treating all of these people with such rudeness and disrespect. When I came across one of the characteristics of love in the Bible, I learned that love is not rude (1 Cor. 13:5).

I could still preach against sin and uphold the truth without being rude. After admitting my inconsistency, I started to delve deeper into my motivation.

Why had I handled people with such harshness? For years, I had convinced myself that I was coming to people "in love" and I did it because I wanted to help people - but did I *really* want to help them? I asked myself a very serious question, *"Do I want to see sinners repent or do I want to see them perish?"*

Do you remember the prophet Jonah? He is usually known for being swallowed by a big fish (Jon. 1:17). However, what follows is very interesting. Jonah ends up preaching to the people at Nineveh telling them to repent (Jon. 3:1-4). When the people heard Jonah's message, they ended up repenting and God forgave them (Jon. 3:10).

Instead of Jonah rejoicing, he was angry at God for not destroying Nineveh (Jon. 4:1-11). When I was honest with myself, I saw that my mentality was a lot like Jonah's.

James and John also wanted to see the wicked perish. They wanted to rain fire down from heaven to consume those who rejected Jesus (Lk. 9:54). Interestingly enough, they attempted to use the prophet Elijah to justify their approach (Lk. 9:51-54). Here is how Jesus responded:

> But He turned and rebuked them, and said, 'You do not know what manner of spirit you are of. For the Son of Man did not come to destroy men's lives but to save them... (Lk. 9:55-56).[19]

In the same way, I didn't know "what manner of spirit I was of." Instead of being a Jonah, James, and John in these instances, I should have been like Hezekiah, Paul, and Abraham. Hezekiah is known as the restoration king. Hezekiah wanted to get things back to the correct way. This is how the Bible describes Hezekiah:

> This is what Hezekiah did throughout Judah, doing what was good and right and faithful before the Lord his God. (2 Chron. 31:20).

I would like to have this kind of resume. The Bible says that Hezekiah trusted in the Lord more than any of his predecessors (2 Kgs. 18:5). After the wicked reign of Ahaz, there was much work to do to get things back to the way they needed to be.

He cleaned out the pagan altars, idols, and temples (2 Kgs. 18:4). He even had the bronze serpent, that Moses had made in the desert, destroyed since the people had turned it into an idol (Num. 21:9; 2 Kgs. 18:4).

Hezekiah was passionate for doing the right thing and he was faithful to God. The temple in Jerusalem was reopened, the Levitical priesthood was reinstated, and the Passover was reinstituted during the reign of Hezekiah (2 Chron. 29:5; 2 Chron. 30:1). Here is where things get interesting.

When Hezekiah was reinstituting the Passover, there was a problem. Many of the Jews were not ceremonially cleansed

---

[19] NKJV

according to the law and they ate the Passover meal contrary to the law. The text says:

> Although most of the many people who came from Ephraim, Manasseh, Issachar and Zebulun had not purified themselves, yet they ate the Passover, contrary to what was written... (2 Chron. 30:18).

Here you have unclean Jews taking the Passover contrary to the law. How do you think Hezekiah handled this situation? Remember, Hezekiah was a man of the law. He was a man of God and he was all about doing things God's way.

Did he rebuke these unclean Jews for eating the Passover contrary to the law? No. Did he condemn them on the spot? No. Did he accuse them of having wrong motives? No. Instead, he prayed that God would accept them if their hearts were in the right place. The text says:

> But Hezekiah prayed for them, saying, 'May the Lord, who is good, pardon everyone who sets their heart on seeking God—the Lord, the God of their ancestors—even if they are not clean according to the rules of the sanctuary. (2 Chron. 30:18-19).

This passage fascinates me. The first thing that really stands out is the love Hezekiah had for these people who were seeking God with their heart. Were these people guilty of violating the laws of the sanctuary? Yes. Were they eating the Passover contrary to the law? Yes. From the perspective of law, they had no hope. They were condemned, legally speaking.

Yet, the way Hezekiah handled these lawbreakers was much different than the way I handled those who disagreed with me. If I am honest with myself, I had no mercy toward those who disagreed with me. I condemned them on the spot. I was their judge and jury. Yet, Hezekiah served as a mediator.

He prayed that God would accept them anyway in spite of their error. The prayer of Hezekiah did not resemble my own prayers. It was as if I had almost found joy in rebuking "sinners." I never once asked God to forgive someone if they were violating His law. Yet, Hezekiah asked that God pardon them and accept them anyway because of their hearts.

In the same way, Abraham interceded for Sodom (Gen. 18:22-33) and Paul said he would give up his own life to save the Jews (Rom. 9:3). God is looking for us to "stand in the gap" for people. Ezek. 22:30 says:

> I looked for someone among them who would build up the wall and stand before me in the gap on behalf of the land so I would not have to destroy it, but I found no one.

Instead of trying to justify my harsh approach and spirit within me like James and John did, I was going to "stand in the gap." I was going to be more like Abraham, Hezekiah, and Paul.

I wanted to truly *love* people. I wanted to have the right motivation. I wanted to actually care about people. I was no longer going to justify my brashness by calling it love. I was no longer going to be inconsistent with how I approached people. I was going to change my approach.

CHAPTER 27
STILL THE SAME

I was determined to change my approach toward other people. I decided to call several people that I had treated very rudely in the past to apologize for my behavior.

I called Dr. West and apologized to him. I called Mr. Collins and apologized to him. I actually ended up contacting around 40 different people to apologize for how I had treated them in the past.

I explained to them that I thought I was doing the right thing at the time. I also told them that while I still had the same belief system, I should have treated them differently.

One man I spoke with, "Mr. Perkins," told me he forgave me and that I needed to learn to forgive myself. He told me that Paul the apostle had committed much worse offenses than I had and he didn't try to track down everyone to apologize to them.

Mr. Perkin's words have been beneficial even to this day. I appreciate him accepting my apology and being so kind to let me know that I just needed to move on and learn from my past.

Not everyone was as forgiving as Mr. Perkins. One man I called, "Mr. Jackson," told me I had caused him unspeakable hurt and anguish and that I will be held responsible for all the chaos and division caused by my actions. I told him that I hope one day he can learn to forgive me because I was truly sorry.

Had I known what I was doing, I would never have done it. I thought that was what I was supposed to be doing for the Lord.

It was a relief to be able to find forgiveness for myself. I now viewed others through the lenses of mercy and grace instead of condemnation and judgment. While I thought the extent of my change had taken place, this would only be the beginning of my change.

In reality, not much had changed in my spirituality. Yes, I was nicer in my approach toward people. Yes, I handled people differently. Yes, I began to use tact. However, I was still very much the same Kevin Pendergrass I had always been in regard to my actual belief system.

This continued for a while until I would begin to re-examine other things in my life. Since I was willing to re-evaluate my approach toward people and saw that I had been wrong on an issue, maybe I was also wrong about other things, too.

I believe the first layer that every person must go through if they are ever going to change is the layer of realization that we are not infallible. We can be wrong. We are not all-knowing, nor do we possess perfect understanding and wisdom.

This new-found humility was very different for me. It was not how I had typically approached situations or my life in general. Granted, there was still a lot of arrogance in me. Yet, I was at least willing to consider some alternatives, especially as it related to some inconsistencies in other areas of my belief system.

While some people noticed minor changes in my behavior during this time, I was still very much influenced by the distinguishing beliefs of my church affiliation. However, I was faced with some inconsistencies in my long-held traditions and theology that would force me into studying more in depth. With my newly opened mind, it was a perfect time for me to re-examine things.

PART 8:
THE QUESTIONS BEGIN

CHAPTER 28
FELLOWSHIP: PARTY OF ONE

Even though my tactfulness had changed, my belief system was still the same. I still saw the same problems, especially as it pertained to unity and fellowship. Jesus prayed for unity and He died for unity.

Instead of living in unity, I experienced division. I would divide and condemn others over frivolous issues. I came to see that this was not the desire of Jesus. Notice the prayer of Jesus:

> I do not pray for these followers only. I pray for those who will put their trust in Me through the teaching they have heard. May they all be as one, Father, as You are in Me and I am in You. May they belong to Us. Then the world will believe that You sent Me (Jn. 17:20-21).

Jesus taught that all believers should seek unity, not division. His spiritual kingdom is designed to include all believers, not just those who see things exactly like I see them. Unity is achieved by working together despite our differences.

I once mistakenly applied Jesus' prayer and other passages such as 1 Cor. 1:10, Amos 3:3, Acts 2:42, and Phil. 2:2 to teach that unity demands perfect agreement in all things. Of course, common sense tells us that no two Christians will ever agree on every biblical matter. But here are two questions that had always bothered me:

1. How are we deciding what issues Christians must agree upon in order to have unity?

2. What issues can Christians agree to disagree upon while still having unity?

Some people call these "salvation issues," some call them "heaven and hell issues," some call them "doctrinal issues," and others call them "fellowship issues."

The idea is the same regardless of terminology. The idea is there are some issues Christians must agree upon in order to have and maintain unity while there are other issues Christians don't have to agree upon in order to have and maintain unity.

Where I came from, just about everything was deemed a "salvation issue" and was worth fighting and dividing over because we believed unity could only be achieved when everyone saw every "doctrinal" issue alike.

However, I had overlooked a glaring problem. Everyone has different ideas and beliefs as to what constitutes a "doctrinal" issue. How was I determining what constituted a so-called "doctrinal issue?"

I kept running into a wall every time I tried to come up with some objective gauge. I asked myself where is it and what is it? If there is an objective gauge, then why can't even two Christians agree on it? Even when I did try to apply different methods of figuring out what is and isn't a doctrinal issue, I saw the blatant inconsistency.

This standard of trying to achieve unity is not a cure for division, it is a prescription for it. I saw how this subjective approach to Scripture could turn anything into a "matter of salvation" or anything into a "matter of opinion" without any rhyme or reason.

This subjective way of studying the Bible is reflective of our post-modernistic society, making issues "essential" and "non-essential" based upon one's own whim and desire.

What I often saw was a preacher who would preach that something was a "salvation issue" only as long as he had enough backing from his church. If he didn't, then he would conveniently label it as a "matter of opinion." However, not everyone was like this.

I was willing to preach what I believed to be the truth, regardless of consequence. I wasn't alone, either. There were many others with whom I associated who didn't care about playing politics or having enough people on their side.

They were willing to "stick to their guns" on what they believed constituted unity no matter what. While this mentality should be applauded, it has its own set of problems.

I had unknowingly made myself out to be the ultimate judge of mankind's salvation. I condemned those who didn't see everything just like me. Sure, I was now nicer about it, but I still had the same belief system.

When I tried to force myself to give an exhaustive list of "salvation issues," I couldn't provide one. How fair is it to claim there is a universal list of "salvation issues" while either not knowing what it is or refusing to provide it?

At one point, I thought I had figured it out and knew every single "doctrinal issue." However, a thought occurred to me: If there is one objective "doctrinal list," shouldn't every single Christian who fellowships with one another have the same identical list?

If I was honest with myself, I had to admit that not even two Christians in fellowship with one another could provide the exact same list.

If everyone's list is different, how can we claim it is universal? The only thing that would be universal about everyone's list is they are universally different. If I were going to teach that unity is dependent upon 100 percent cognitive "doctrinal agreement," then I was obligated to provide the following:

1. I had to provide where this method of unity is taught in Scripture.
2. I had to provide the objective and biblical gauge that distinguishes between a matter of "opinion" and a matter of "doctrine/fellowship."
3. I had to provide the full and completed detailed list of "doctrines" necessary for unity about which all must agree.
4. I had to honestly ask myself why even two Christians couldn't agree upon an exhaustive list.

My whole belief about unity had been presumed. I couldn't even answer one of these questions consistently, much less all four of them.

This whole time I had believed that my approach to unity was objective, but in reality, it was nothing but subjective postmodernism.

To hammer this out even further, if you still believe unity is dependent upon 100 percent cognitive doctrinal agreement, then please answer the following questions honestly:

1. Do you believe every single person with whom you fellowship has the exact same list of doctrinal/fellowship issues that you also identify as doctrinal/fellowship issues?
2. Do you believe every single person agrees with you on every single issue you deem to be a doctrinal/fellowship issue?
3. Could you still fellowship someone if their list of fellowship issues differed from yours in any way?
4. If someone happened to disagree with you on just one issue you deem a doctrinal/fellowship issue, would you remain consistent with your view of unity by

withdrawing/disfellowshipping every single person who disagrees with you?[20]

Here are the absurd conclusions that this belief demands: (1) Everyone must have the exact same universal "essential doctrine/fellowship issue" list. (2) Everyone must agree and hold to the same beliefs on the list. (That means not only must we agree on what we think every single "fellowship issue is," but we must also have the exact same belief on every single one of those issues).

Finally, if someone has a different list than you have on even just one point or if they have a different view on any of the points on the list, then that person is someone who can't be fellowshipped.

When I was completely honest with this approach, I came to only one conclusion: The only person I could fellowship was myself! At the time, I didn't know what constituted unity, but I knew that I could no longer teach a standard of unity that is unbiblical and subjective.

If the standard of unity I had believed for years was wrong, then could there be other things that I had missed in my Christianity? I knew I had approached people incorrectly, but had I been viewing the Bible with a wrong approach, too?

---

[20] 1 Cor. 5:1-12; 2 Thess. 3:14; 2 Jn. 9

CHAPTER 29
UNDERTONES OF ASCETICISM

At this point in my Christianity, I literally had no idea how I should be approaching unity and Christian fellowship. I knew that the way I had been approaching unity was incorrect, but I didn't know the correct way. I didn't know the answer, but I knew what wasn't the answer.

This became even more apparent to me when I was a guest speaker at a particular congregation. When I arrived, one of the members informed me that the church was in the middle of several splits after being in constant debate about a topic.

They were hoping I could give my input to help with the situation. The heated debate centered around the subject of alcohol and what the Bible says about it. All agreed that getting drunk is a sin.[21]

Yet, some believed that drinking alcohol, even in moderation, is a sin. Therefore, the first splinter group was the group who believed it was wrong to drink alcohol in moderation. They condemned all others who disagreed with them.

However, another debate arose within this new group. While all in this group believed that drinking alcohol in moderation is a sin, some believed that it is a sin to go to any restaurants that have open bars.

---

[21] Rom. 13:13, Gal. 5:19-21, I Tim. 3:1-7, I Pet. 4:3; Eph. 5:18

Therefore, the second splinter group was the group who believed it is a sin to go to any restaurants that have open bars. They condemned those who disagreed with them.

From this group arose even another debate. While all in this group believed that going to any restaurants that have open bars is a sin, some believed it is a sin to go to any restaurants that serve alcohol, even if they don't have an open bar.

Therefore, the third group was formed who believed it is a sin to go to any restaurants that serve alcohol. They condemned those who disagreed with them.

Finally, one last debate arose from this group. While all in this group believed that going to any restaurant that serves alcohol is sinful, some believed it is a sin to go to any establishment, whatsoever, that sells alcohol.

Therefore, a final group was formed who believed it is a sin to go to any establishment that sells alcohol. They condemned those who disagreed with them.

Interestingly enough, this last group justified buying gasoline at convenient stores as long as you didn't go inside the establishment and they also justified buying groceries at grocery stores as long as they didn't go down the alcohol aisle.

Throughout the progression of these convictions, you probably noticed that each new group that formed condemned the other groups. The problem wasn't with the personal convictions themselves, but rather the binding of these personal convictions on others.

If one group felt it was better not to eat at a restaurant that serves alcohol, then by all means they shouldn't do it. However, the problem begins when one group forces their own laws on others.

What I noticed in this real-life example is that the stricter each group became, the more righteous and superior each group saw themselves. Of course, this mentality isn't limited to just alcohol.

This can be done with practically any subject, belief, or practice. As I began my study down this road, I saw how Paul dealt with this same kind of harmful approach and mentality in the book of Colossians. Paul said:

> Since you died with Christ to the elemental spiritual forces of this world, why, as though you still belonged to the world, do you submit to its rules: "Do not handle! Do not taste! Do not touch!"? These rules, which have to do with things that are all destined to perish with use, are based on merely human commands and teachings. Such regulations indeed have an appearance of wisdom, with their self-imposed worship, their false humility and their harsh treatment of the body, but they lack any value in restraining sensual indulgence. (Col. 2:20-23).

Paul was dealing with the false doctrine of asceticism. Asceticism is "characterized by severe self-discipline and abstention from all forms of indulgence, typically for religious reasons."[22]

The false teachers in Colossae had created their own system of religious regulations and then imposed them on others. They felt any indulgence of the flesh was sinful.

They combined some of the Old Testament laws with their own traditions and philosophies to come up with their rules while claiming they are God's rules. Even Paul admitted that these rules had the appearance of wisdom (Col. 2:23).

Paul taught that all of these man-made rules focused on the external (Col. 2:21, 23). Paul probably quoted the false teachers' own sayings when he summarized their belief system of "Do not touch, do not taste, do not handle" (Col. 2:22). His point is that these sorts of rules cannot deal with spiritual heart problems.

---

[22] www.oxforddictionaries.com, "Asceticism."

Sure, you can keep all the rules you want and even add your own rules, but that doesn't change a thing if your heart is not in the right place.

This whole time, had I been enforcing my own rules while unintentionally believing them to be the principles of God? Was I the one who had been guilty of binding the traditions of men?[23] Had I been guilty of approaching Scripture with subtle undertones of asceticism?

---

[23] Col. 2:8, 22-23; Mk. 7:7-8; Mt. 15:6-9

CHAPTER 30
WHAT IS SIN?

I used to toss the word "sin" out left and right. It didn't really matter what it was; I would accuse anyone of being in sin if they didn't agree with my biblical "doctrine." What is sin? The word "sin" means "missing the mark."[24] In order for someone to miss a mark, there must first be a mark.

When God told Adam and Eve not to eat from the tree of knowledge of good and evil, He was laying forth a mark. They missed the mark when they violated God's command (Gen. 2:17). The Bible says:

> And where there is no law there is no transgression. (Rom. 4:15).

We sin when we violate God's law (1 Jn. 3:4). If we have not been given a law in regard to a subject or practice, then we have no right to bind our own traditions on others as law.

An example of this taking place can be found in Acts 15. Here, we find some Jewish Christians teaching that in order to be saved, you had to be circumcised and keep the law (Acts 15:1). Paul corrected this belief by saying:

> Since we have heard that some who went out from us have troubled you with words, unsettling your souls, saying, 'You must be circumcised and keep the law'—to whom we gave no such commandment. (Acts 15:24).[25]

---

[24] https://biblehub.com/greek/266.htm. Hamartia.
[25] NKJV

While there was nothing wrong with being circumcised (Acts 16:3; Gal. 5:6), these men were teaching that you *must* be circumcised in order to be saved. This is where they were wrong.

They were binding practices that God had not bound as law (Mt. 18:18). They didn't have a right to enforce their own rules on others if God hadn't given a command on the matter. Paul and Jesus both dealt constantly with those who wanted to bind the traditions of men.[26]

I was very familiar with both the Old and New Testament passages that teach against the dangers of adding to or taking away from God's word.[27] I must have quoted Paul hundreds of times when He instructed not to go beyond that which is written (1 Cor. 4:6).

I would often warn others against teaching another gospel (Gal. 6:1-10). I would encourage everyone to make sure they are abiding in the doctrine of Christ (2 Jn. 9).

Yet, was I the very one adding to God's words by adding laws not found in the Bible? The questions continued in my mind: Was I the one going beyond what was written by making additional rules? Was I the one teaching another gospel by binding regulations on others that aren't found in Scripture? Instead of protecting it, was I actually destroying the gospel?

---

[26] Col. 2:15-23; Mk. 7:1-23; Mt. 15:1-9; Mt. 23:13-30
[27] Deut. 4:2; 12:32; 5:32; Prov. 4:27; 30:6; Rev. 22:18-19

CHAPTER 31
WRONG, BUT NOT SIN

I had always equated being wrong on a biblical matter with the same thing as being in sin. In other words, if you are wrong about any biblical subject, then that is sin. If you have a "false" view about any biblical topic, then you are a "false teacher."

While this sounds good in theory, I was shocked to find that this is not the case. As we learned from the last chapter, sin is not when you are wrong about something. Sin occurs when you are in violation of God's law.

Let me demonstrate this biblical concept. During the first century, one of the great controversies among some Christians centered around the eating of meats that had been sacrificed to idols.

Some believed it was wrong to buy and eat meats if the meat had been sacrificed to a pagan god. Others believed there was nothing wrong with eating meats sacrificed to idols.

What was the answer to the dilemma in which these Christians were faced? Paul begins by establishing the truth that there is nothing wrong with eating meats sacrificed to idols (1 Cor. 8:4). Remember, there is always truth.

However, did that mean that all of those who thought it was wrong to eat meats sacrificed to idols now had to agree with Paul before they could all have unity? No. Did they have to repent of holding to a "false" view before they could be considered faithful Christians? No. Did it mean that division was inevitable if everyone didn't agree? No, it did not.

In fact, notice the words of Paul when addressing this issue:

> But not everyone possesses this knowledge. Some people are still so accustomed to idols that when they eat sacrificial food they think of it as having been sacrificed to a god, and since their conscience is weak, it is defiled. But food does not bring us near to God; we are no worse if we do not eat, and no better if we do. Be careful, however, that the exercise of your rights does not become a stumbling block to the weak. For if someone with a weak conscience sees you, with all your knowledge, eating in an idol's temple, won't that person be emboldened to eat what is sacrificed to idols? So this weak brother or sister, for whom Christ died, is destroyed by your knowledge. (1 Cor. 8:7-11).

Paul's point was simple: Everyone is not going to have the same knowledge on every issue (1 Cor. 8:7). That doesn't mean there is not a correct interpretation to every issue; it just means I won't always possess it on every conceivable biblical matter. To claim otherwise would mean that I am claiming to be omniscient.

Paul knew that unity did not demand that everyone agree on this issue about meats sacrificed to idols. Paul also knew that in order to be considered a faithful Christian, you didn't have to be right about everything.

That doesn't mean that we shouldn't strive to be right about everything (Phil. 3:14-16). However, unless we are perfect with perfect knowledge and perfect application of that knowledge, we will never be able to be right about everything.

While there was nothing wrong in eating meats sacrificed to idols, many believed it was a sin. Instead of forcing them to agree with the truth, Paul said to let it go for the sake of unity and love since God had not given a law on the matter of meats sacrificed to idols.

This means that while many Christians held the wrong belief about meats sacrificed to idols, they were not in sin. Paul taught that being wrong is not the same thing as being in sin.

This becomes an extremely interesting text considering that in this same letter Paul had earlier told the Corinthians that there were to be no divisions among them (1 Cor. 1:10).

Yet, here he is a few chapters later telling them that they don't have to agree. He is telling them that it is OK to be divided on this issue while remaining unified in Christ (1 Cor. 8:1-13).

When Paul said we are to be of the same mind, he didn't mean all Christians had to agree on every single Bible issue to be unified. When Paul spoke about unity, he was speaking about our unity in Jesus Christ as our Savior (1 Cor. 1:10). He was referencing our identity in Christ (1 Cor. 1:16-17). Paul wasn't speaking of every single conceivable Bible topic or issue.

On the contrary, Paul taught that it is OK at times to disagree on spiritual matters (Rom. 14:1-23; 1 Cor. 8:1-13). Yet, when it comes to Jesus, we are to be unified under the banner of Jesus Christ as Savior as we trust in His redemptive work on the cross (1 Cor. 15:1-4; Phil. 2:5-11). Paul made this plain when he said:

> For I resolved to know nothing while I was with you except Jesus Christ and him crucified. (1 Cor. 2:2).

> Now, brothers and sisters, I want to remind you of the gospel I preached to you, which you received and on which you have taken your stand. By this gospel you are saved, if you hold firmly to the word I preached to you. Otherwise, you have believed in vain. For what I received I passed on to you as of first importance: that Christ died for our sins according to the Scriptures, that he was buried, that he was raised on the third day according to the Scriptures. (1 Cor. 15:1-4).

Instead of making Jesus the focus of Christian unity, I was coming to the undeniable conclusion that I had made my own contrived belief system the focus of unity. This started to become a very scary and uncomfortable time in my life.

My whole foundation for fellowship and unity was being shaken to the core. During this time, only a handful of people knew I was having all of these questions and struggles.

My mentor, Mr. Williams, told me he once had similar struggles, too, but that I would figure out everything. He told me I "already had the truth" and I didn't need to question so much. However, when I went to him with my questions, he admitted that he couldn't answer them.

The man who once answered my questions years ago so seamlessly was now at a loss for words. He even told me that he didn't want to discuss those issues with me.

One of my co-workers, "Mike," told me that he agreed with me on many of these points, but he never ended up pursuing it. On the other hand, my wife Bethany, and a couple of my best friends, Brandon & Terry, wanted to "grab the bull by the horns" and figure out this thing. It was at this point I started to do a lot more questioning. I was willing to be "all in" and to follow the evidence regardless of where it led me.

CHAPTER 32
THE GOLDILOCKS COMPLEX

Before I started down this new pursuit of truth, I wanted to make sure I was doing it in the right way. You may recall the children's story of Goldilocks and the Three Little Bears.

When Goldilocks ate the porridge, one bowl was too hot and the other was too cold. Yet, one bowl was "jusssst right."

Up until this point, I had viewed my Christianity as being not too far to the right and not too far to the left. I was "jusssst right." I had what I like to call the "Goldilocks complex."

It feels good to be convinced we are "balanced," doesn't it? This is how I always had approached Christianity. There is a sense in which this gives us superficial peace. We have a feeling of comfort that we are where we need to be if we believe we aren't "too far" to the left or "too far" to the right.

I used to speak of truth being in the middle of both extremes. To demonstrate this point, I used to draw a line and say that a Christian should always strive to be somewhere in the middle because truth is in the middle of both extremes.

I once talked about avoiding the "pendulum swing" mentality. This is when someone will go from one extreme position about an issue to the exact opposite position.

Human nature has a tendency when abandoning one belief to jump all the way to the other side. I didn't want to do that.

I didn't want to go from one extreme to another. But I started to be mindful of my "Goldilocks complex." What do we even mean when we say the "other extreme?" I asked myself if going to the other extreme is always wrong. I noticed how Paul went from killing Christians to bringing people to Christ (Acts 26:9-11). This was an extreme change. Would any Christian dare claim that Paul was wrong for his "pendulum swing?"

Furthermore, claiming that something is extreme doesn't make it wrong. Atheists claim that believing a man died for the sins of the world and was raised from the dead is about as extreme as it gets, after all! Does that mean I shouldn't be a Christian?

While I once claimed that truth is in the middle, I now wondered what I even meant by that. The middle of what? Where had I gotten this abstract and post-modernistic idea that truth is somewhere in the middle?

The problem is that truth is sometimes at the other extreme from where you are standing (as was the case with Paul).

If an atheist believed that truth was in the middle and Christianity was at the other extreme, would he need to become an agnostic in order to avoid going to the other extreme? In this scenario, a Christian would argue that truth wasn't "in the middle," but rather, truth was on the other side. The "pendulum swing" was the way to go in this instance.

I realized that if I were going to go in search of the truth, I should try not to avoid going to the other extreme just to avoid the other extreme. In doing so, I could be avoiding truth. Ironically, always avoiding the "other extreme" is, in and of itself, an extreme.

I concluded that instead of analyzing who holds what positions or beliefs and trying to make sure I am "in the middle," I was only going to concern myself with researching the evidence and staking my convictions where the Bible led me.

It is a subjective claim when one says they are "balanced" in their religious belief system. After all, you will always be able to find someone who holds a more "liberal" position and a more "conservative" position than you.

Someone will always be to your right and to your left. From this perspective, everyone could claim they are "balanced." That is why it is mere rhetoric to claim that one should always strive to be in "the middle."

I didn't care about church politics. I didn't care about what others would think about me. I didn't care about having the approval of a certain group of people. No, I cared about finding the truth and seeking Jesus.

I was going to break down every barrier, both internally and externally, to accomplish this. Before I could find answers, there were still many questions. Before I could learn truth, I had to unlearn my error.

PART 9:
LIVING IN FEAR

CHAPTER 33
FEAR OF BEING WRONG

Having more questions than answers is not a good feeling. The feeling of realizing I had been wrong on several things when I thought I had been right really rocked my world.

I now knew what it was like to believe something to be true, yet be totally wrong. I could relate to how Jacob felt when he realized Joseph was still alive after believing he had been dead for years (Gen. 45:25-27) or when Paul realized he was wrong after he had been persecuting Christians (Acts 26:9). I discovered that conviction is not always the same thing as truth.

Once I accepted all of this, I was faced with a terrifying thought. If I could be wrong on something, then what if I am currently wrong on an issue that could keep me out of heaven? What if I am currently doing something (or not doing something) that will cause me to be lost?

The thought of being wrong is scary when the stakes are high. The eternal fate of my soul is certainly a high stake. Therefore, I was in constant fear of being wrong on any given biblical topic.

I had been very arrogant and thought I had everything figured out up until this point. When I realized I wasn't all-knowing, this caused me great fear and doubt. The more I preached, the more I realized many other people had this same fear and doubt, too.

Years ago, I had finished preaching a lesson on grace as a visiting speaker at a church in Texas. After I concluded my lesson, I had a nice woman named "Janice" come up to me with tears in her eyes. Janice asked if she could speak to me for a moment. Our presumed short conversation turned into a long discussion.

She exemplified all of the traits you could imagine that a faithful Christian would have based upon what she told me. She grew up in a loving, Christian family. She became a Christian as a teenager. She never rebelled as a child, she saved herself for marriage, and she had stayed the course as we often would say at church.

She went to church services every time the doors were opened and she studied her Bible and prayed daily. She had a great relationship with her parents. She had a wonderful godly marriage. She had raised godly children who had godly spouses. She visited the sick. She gave to the poor. She had compassion for those less fortunate than herself, and she had brought others to Christ. Yet, she doubted whether or not she was "right" with God.

Janice told me she realized she could never have it all figured out no matter how much she studied. She always doubted whether or not she was really accepted by God. In fact, the more she studied, the more she doubted, especially when she would learn something new. "What if I have missed something?" she asked.

She told me that since she wasn't all-knowing, how could she know for sure she had figured out everything she was supposed to figure out in order to go to heaven? After all, if you are ignorantly wrong on an issue, then you wouldn't know it.

Her constant doubt about the possibility of being ignorantly wrong kept her from having assurance of her salvation.

What Janice didn't know was that I felt the exact same way. Of course, instead of being vulnerable with her and telling her my doubts, I just quoted her some passages. These were my "go-to" passages that I quoted her:

> This is how love is made complete among us so that we will have confidence on the day of judgment: In this world we are like Jesus. There is no fear in love. But perfect love drives out fear,

because fear has to do with punishment. The one who fears is not made perfect in love. We love because he first loved us. (1 Jn. 4:17-19).

I write these things to you who believe in the name of the Son of God so that you may know that you have eternal life. (1 Jn. 5:13).

Therefore, there is now no condemnation for those who are in Christ Jesus... (Rom. 8:1).

Since the children have flesh and blood, he too shared in their humanity so that by his death he might break the power of him who holds the power of death—that is, the devil— and free those who all their lives were held in slavery by their fear of death (Heb. 2:14-15).

I told her that, according to these Bible passages, she can know she has eternal life and she shouldn't fear death or the judgment. Little did she know I had the same questions, fears, and doubts.

The truth of the matter is that when I strived for humility,[28] I lost confidence, too. To me, it was as if humility and confidence were polar opposites. Up until then, I believed I was saved because I was confident that I was right about everything.

Now, I was humble enough to admit that I could be wrong which meant I was insecure about whether or not I was actually right with God. How could I admit I could be wrong while remaining confident in my salvation?

At times, I wished I could have gone back to the way things were when I had deceived myself into thinking I had everything figured out, but it was too late to go back. My eyes had been opened and I knew my own fallibility.

Questions flooded my mind. What if I were a false teacher and just didn't know it? What if I had come to wrong conclusions on other matters about which I wasn't aware? What if matters I thought

---

[28] Phil. 2:3; Rom. 12:16; Ja. 4:6

were small were actually big? What if, what if, what if? The questions were endless and the answers were nowhere in sight.

I often reminded myself how God handled disobedience. Take Nadab and Abihu for example (Lev. 10:1-7). They were the two oldest sons of Aaron (Num. 3:2-3). They sinned by offering profane fire to the Lord. As soon as they did this, fire went out from the Lord and killed them.

Another example is found with Uzzah and the ark of the covenant (2 Sam. 6:1-7;1 Chron. 13:9-12). The people were commanded not to touch the ark of the covenant (Num. 4:15).

As the ark of the covenant was being transported, the ark started to fall as the oxen stumbled; and Uzzah reached down to grab the ark so it wouldn't fall to the ground (2 Sam. 6:6). As soon as he touched the ark, God struck Uzzah dead (2 Sam. 6:7). What seemed to be nothing but a knee jerk reaction was punished by death.

I would often say that when God says something, He means it. Think about Num. 15:32-36 when God commanded that a man be stoned because he violated the Sabbath law by picking up sticks on the Sabbath. I knew that God takes obedience and disobedience seriously. I wanted to follow God and believed I was, but I had been wrong in the past.

What if I was wrong on something else and didn't know it? I was very familiar with what Jesus said in Mt. 7:21-23. I knew there would be many people who would be condemned who thought they did the right thing. What if I were one of those individuals who thought I was following God, but really was not?

How would I even know the difference? If I was ignorantly doing something wrong, I obviously wouldn't know it because I would be ignorant to the fact. With my understanding of Scripture at that time, I was left with the following conclusions:

1. I am not infallible in my study.

2. I could be ignorantly wrong on issues.

3. If I were ignorantly wrong on an issue, I wouldn't know it.

4. If I am ignorantly wrong on my belief about a biblical issue, this means I could be lost.

With these conclusions, where was my hope? How could I, or anyone for that matter, have any confidence in their salvation?

If my confidence in salvation was dependent upon me getting everything right and I could always be ignorantly doing something wrong, then there is no scenario in which I could ever be confident in my salvation. Salvation, therefore, becomes a toss-up even for the most faithful person.

Did God leave us with this kind of hopeless "hope?" Had God given me a belief system that was this shaky? Let me remind you, I knew that the Bible *says* I can know I am saved and be confident, but that didn't make any sense with my understanding of Christianity at the time. I was left wondering if I was going to always have this constant fear of my salvation.

CHAPTER 34
BLURRED VISION

Aside from all of my questions about ignorance, confidence, and salvation, I started to do some self-reflection when it came to my own personal life. In addition to not even knowing if I was saved, my approach to Christianity at that time caused me to conceal my own secret sins instead of confessing and confronting them.

As humans, we want to present ourselves in the most positive light. Especially now with social media, it is very easy to give a perception of our lives that may not match up to the day-to-day realities.

It is easier than ever to portray ourselves as someone we may not be in real life. I'm not talking about willful deception. Rather, I'm talking about idealism. If we are not careful, we can give a false perception about ourselves as Christians. Instead of letting people know who we really are, we conceal the parts we don't want others to see.

We can find ourselves caring more about reputation than character. The scribes and Pharisees were masters at looking great on the outside but concealing who they really were on the inside. Jesus said:

> Woe to you, teachers of the law and Pharisees, you hypocrites! You are like whitewashed tombs, which look beautiful on the outside but on the inside are full of the bones of the dead and everything unclean. In the same way, on the outside you appear to people as righteous but on the inside you are full of hypocrisy and wickedness. (Mt. 23:27-28).

I had trusted in myself for so long that when I realized just how weak I was and had been, I didn't know what to do anymore. I was afraid to let anyone see anything that could be perceived as a weakness.

I was too afraid to talk about my weaknesses because I was unsure how I would be received. Therefore, it was easier to conceal them within my pride and arrogance instead of revealing them in humility and vulnerability. Unfortunately, when we do this, it will always lead to hypocrisy.

Being honest with ourselves isn't easy, especially when it comes to our own struggles and sins. Jesus had much to say about making sure our own backyard is taken care of before we complain about our neighbor's (Gal. 6:4-5; 2 Cor. 13:5). I used to be more worried about the "specks" in everyone else's eyes than the big plank in my own (Mt. 7:3-5). I had blurred vision.

One of the reasons why it is so easy to judge other people is because it takes the focus off of ourselves and our own weaknesses. If everyone is talking about someone else, then I won't have to worry about them talking about me and my struggles. Therefore, it is very easy to ignore our own sins while shedding light on the sins of others.

The truth of the matter is that we all have planks in our eye at times. Therefore, we need to be vulnerable and honest about our own faults.

When we think about the apostle Paul, we don't usually think about a weak man who struggled with doing the right thing. We tend to emphasize his godly traits. However, even Paul struggled with sin and he was honest with himself about it (Rom. 7:13-15).

For years, I chose not to be honest with my sinfulness. Instead, I was in denial about my own secret sin while condemning everyone else. I thought I was so much better than everyone else. I look back at the story about the Pharisee and tax collector and realize that I had the same mentality of the Pharisee. Jesus said:

> To some who were confident of their own righteousness and looked down on everyone else, Jesus told this parable: 'Two men went up to the temple to pray, one a Pharisee and the other a tax collector. The Pharisee stood by himself and prayed: 'God, I thank you that I am not like other people—robbers, evildoers, adulterers—or even like this tax collector. I fast twice a week and give a tenth of all I get.' 'But the tax collector stood at a distance. He would not even look up to heaven, but beat his breast and said, 'God, have mercy on me, a sinner.' 'I tell you that this man, rather than the other, went home justified before God. For all those who exalt themselves will be humbled, and those who humble themselves will be exalted. (Lk. 18:9-14).

Instead of realizing my own sinfulness and humanity, I wanted to brag about all the wonderful things I had done in the name of God. I didn't come humbly and honestly before God. I allowed myself to be blinded by my own plank.

For many years, I had previously struggled with the sin of pornography. It was a private sin. I didn't want to let anyone know about this sin because I didn't want anyone to think less of me or use it against me. What made it worse was that this was during the time in which I was very judgmental in my approach to Christianity.

I even remember one time when I had preached a sermon about modesty and then later during the same day looked up pornography on my computer. Talk about a hypocrite! Here I was condemning others, yet I was completely blind to my own sin.

I knew what I had done wasn't right. I knew it was a sin. Yet, believe it or not, my approach to Christianity had enabled me to keep looking up pornography in a way where I felt justified. With the way I viewed Christianity, all I had to do was ritualistically ask God to forgive me and I was as "good as new." Each time I would vow to never do it again only to do it again and again and again. I was trusting in law to save me by saying a quick prayer while justifying my own lust of the eyes.

At that point in my life, I believed living a Christian life virtually meant living perfectly with absolutely no sin. So, how did I deal with sin? Well, I felt justified as long as I said a prayer asking God to forgive me. However, now my mentality had changed toward my sin and myself. I was now feeling more condemned than ever because I was more vulnerable and honest with myself and my past sins.

Thankfully, with the help of God and others, I had defeated the sin of pornography, but during this stage of my life I found myself feeling completely condemned with no hope as I looked back at my self-justification.

Not only did I believe that I might be doing something ignorantly wrong that could keep me out of heaven, I now saw how bad I had been and how I had justified my own sin. Furthermore, I had acted this way when I was condemning everyone else.

My faulty approach to Christianity had led me to the point where I had been an arrogant hypocrite. How could I have missed this? How could I have had such self-righteousness? How could I have not seen this?

My blurred vision and warped approach to Scripture had enabled me to live a life of self-denial, arrogance, self-justification, and ruthlessness toward others.

I couldn't keep doing what I was doing. I couldn't keep living the way I was living, I couldn't keep preaching what I had been preaching, and I couldn't keep approaching unity the way I had been approaching unity. I was truly at a loss.

I knew all the things about which I had been wrong, but I had no clue as to where I needed to go next in order to be right. With all of these questions and doubts in my mind, I didn't know everything I needed to do in order to change; however, one thing I knew I had to do was resign from my job.

CHAPTER 35
I RESIGN FROM MY JOB

By the middle of 2014, I knew a change had to take place in my life. I didn't feel like I could continue being the director of the ministry with which I had worked since graduating from preaching school. As much as I loved the job, I knew I was at a much different place in my beliefs than when I first took the job.

I no longer held to many of the dogmatic conclusions that I did at one time. It wasn't so much that I rejected all my former practices or beliefs. Rather, I now refused to bind all of my beliefs on other believers.

I couldn't keep preaching an approach to unity that I no longer believed. I wasn't going to draw lines that I didn't believe should be drawn. Therefore, in October of 2014, I officially resigned from my position as director of the program. Below is an extract from a letter I wrote after I resigned:

> There were multiple reasons why I decided to resign. To go ahead and get the inevitable question out of the way; no, I wasn't fired. I wasn't 'asked to resign.' This decision was my own and one that had been in the making for some time. I feel that too many preachers forget who their real boss is. Who do we really work for? Instead of working with the church and working for God, I feel that too many preachers work for the church. At times, I experienced preachers compromising intellectual integrity for the sake of a paycheck. I had conversations with preachers who told me what they really believed about a doctrinal matter. Yet, they would then explain to me how they could never express how they really felt because of fear of what the congregation would say or do.

I saw how 'church' was all too often a game for many preachers and Christians. What is so sad was that I was caught up in this game for a period of time. I was guilty as charged. I was a 'defender of the faith,' going along seeing how many 'false teachers' I could knock off. All of the while, I didn't realize the true damage I was doing. We in the brotherhood have not created an environment of openness and honesty. Instead, we have created an environment of 'don't ask, don't tell.'

Christians refuse to express their views to their preachers and pastors out of fear of what may happen whereas preachers and pastors refuse to express their views to congregants because of fear of what may happen. So, what happens? We keep our mouths shut and 'play church' while quickly drawing lines and marking those who challenge us or do not immediately agree with everything we believe. The young people are the first to see these inconsistences and hypocrisies. Sadly, I look back in remorse readily admitting that I have been part of the problem.

In my studies I have had questions about some things. I have looked at some of my own doctrinal positions and realized the lack of biblical argumentation for them. I have noted my own arrogance and belief in my own infallibility and I am doing everything I can to change that. I saw some inconsistencies in my own beliefs on certain issues and had questions that I couldn't answer. Lord willing, I hope to post many of my questions in the future on my blog. I would like to share what I find to be inconsistencies and hope to challenge your thinking as you challenge mine.

Many were shocked at my resignation. During the months leading up to this, I tried to keep this as quiet as possible. I knew the backlash that I would receive when people started finding out I was no longer binding some of my views. I knew I would now be looked upon as the enemy by many of my contemporaries. Fortunately, I wasn't on this journey alone. I thank God daily for my wonderful wife and two of my best friends, Brandon and Terry, who fought this good fight with me.

When word started circulating that I had resigned, many people became very curious. When they started to find out that I no longer held to many of the beliefs of my church affiliation, I received e-mails, phone calls, text messages, letters, and personal visits.

People I had never heard of were coming out of the woodwork to express their disappointment in me. While some were much kinder than others in their approach, the message was the same: I needed to repent and "come back" to the truth. In their minds, I had left the truth.

I clearly let it be known that my faith was not wavering in God and Jesus Christ. I told them that I believe the Bible, I believe in God, and I believe in Jesus Christ. It was not the true faith I was abandoning, rather, it was the traditions of men.

I was no longer going to draw lines where God never drew them. Of course, they were not going to have any of that. They were too busy trying to bring me back to the way I once was. One person even sent me one of my old articles to read hoping it would change me.

It was at this time that the majority of my friends, my acquaintances, and even my mentor, Mr. Williams, decided to part ways with me. In their eyes, I was now a false teacher. Their reason? I was a false teacher to them because I wasn't willing to *condemn* all the same believers that they condemned (and who I once condemned to hell).

Therefore, they drew a line between us because I wasn't willing to draw all of their lines. After resigning, I knew that things were not going to be easy for a while, but I didn't really know just how tough things were going to be for me.

CHAPTER 36
LOSING MY IDENTITY

When I resigned from my position, I became very self-absorbed and spent way too much time feeling sorry for myself. I had a pity party for one. After I resigned from my job, my wife and I moved in with my parents for several months until we could get back on our feet.

A few months prior to this, I had a stable life, owned my own house, directed a ministry, and had a secure job. Now, I found myself having lost most of my friends, having no direction, living with my parents, and jobless. I didn't have any formal education in anything other than preaching. I found that outside of church work, a preaching certificate won't get you very far in the way of a job.

I considered looking at another preaching job, but I didn't want to get back into church work at that time, and quite frankly, I didn't know where to turn even if I had wanted to do church work. I had completely lost my identity and I needed more time to find out where I actually stood with my spiritual beliefs.

Furthermore, my wife and I found ourselves under constant attack from my former contemporaries and other churches in which I once worked. I allowed this to consume me. I received very hateful letters, e-mails, and text messages condemning me to hell. In reality, I was only getting the same medicine I had dished out for years.

Some of these messages came from people I knew, some from people I didn't, and others were anonymous. Instead of rising above and moving on, I played the victim during this time. Thankfully, God always gives us what we need when we need it. My wife is my rock. She especially strengthened me during this period. While I was the one allowing the insults to affect me, she, on the other hand, exemplified much more faith in God and His plan than I did at the time.

I found myself becoming very angry and bitter. Instead of demonstrating this love and grace I claimed I had found, I still hadn't truly changed. Sure, I had changed my mind on several positions and certainly wasn't the same person I once was; yet, I still acted the same in many ways. The main change still hadn't taken place inside of me, yet. I was still "missing the forest for the trees." I was still looking at the Bible as itemized issues. I was still trying to gain God's favor through my own works. As much as I wanted to, I couldn't connect the dots.

So, I decided to go back to the fundamentals. I wanted to start from the beginning. It was during this humbling time that I would rediscover (and perhaps truly discover) the real meaning and depth of the gospel.

PART 10:
BACK TO THE FUNDAMENTALS

CHAPTER 37
UNDERSTANDING GOD'S HOLINESS AND LOVE

Up until this point in my life, the focus of my Christianity had been on myself. It was about me. Yet, I realized that Christianity is not about *my* righteousness before God. Christianity is about Christ's righteousness before me.

As an accountable human, I finally realized the great sin dilemma with which I was faced.[29] The Bible teaches that we have all sinned and we all fall short of the glory of God (Rom. 3:23). As discussed in Chapter 30, sin is missing the mark (1 Jn. 3:4). It is violating God's standard of living found in His word, the Bible (Rom. 4:15; 10:17).

Here is the problem with sin: The wages of sin is death (Rom. 6:23). When we sin, not only do we incur a death penalty, but that sin separates us from God (Isa. 59:1-2). God says that my righteousness is nothing but filthy rags (Isa. 64:6).

That means even on my best day, I don't even begin to come close to meeting God's standard. I can attempt to deny my own sinfulness, but the Bible says if we say we have no sin, then we are only deceiving ourselves (1 Jn. 1:8). We cannot find righteousness through our own works (Rom. 3:10).

While I had known these facts for years, I never truly understood them. This whole time I was trying to approach God

---

[29] Eccl. 7:29; Ezek. 28:15; Isa. 7:15-16; Rom. 9:11; Deut. 1:34-39; Ja. 1:14-15; Gen. 8:21

with my righteousness. It was no wonder I was failing miserably. My righteousness is nothing. God is on the other side of the spectrum. The Bible describes God as being a holy God (Isa. 6:3; Rev. 4:8).

This means God can't stop being holy any more than He can stop being righteous. It is part of Him. Holiness is part of God's nature.[30] Since God is holy, that means He is absolutely free from sin and cannot be in the presence of sin. Notice the following verse about God:

> Your eyes are too pure to look on evil; you cannot tolerate wrongdoing. (Hab. 1:13).

The holiness of God hates sin and cannot tolerate it.[31] It is for this reason that even our righteousness looks like filthy rags to God (Isa. 64:6).

Once we sin, we have separated ourselves from God and there is nothing we, in and of ourselves, can do to ever gain back our fellowship with God. This is why any law system renders mankind hopeless before God. James says:

> For whoever keeps the whole law and yet stumbles at just one point is guilty of breaking all of it. (Ja. 2:10).

When we mess up once and sin, that is it. No more second chances. No more hope. We can never do enough to gain God's favor back once we have lost it. Our works are worthless. No one is righteous, no not one (Rom. 3:10).

The holiness of God is how we understand God's justice. God's holiness determines what is intrinsically right and wrong. It is God's holiness that sets the standard. It is our sin that separates us from God and it is God's holiness that demands we stay separated

---

[30] Josh. 24:19-20; 1 Pet. 1:15-16; Psa. 25:8; Lev. 11:45; Psa. 18:25-26; 1 Jn. 3:3; Psa. 24:3-4; Col. 1:22
[31] Job. 34:10-12; Ja. 1:13; Psa. 5:4; Isa. 59:2

because of our sinfulness. Since we sinned, we must account for it. This is fair. This is justice. This is the holiness of God.

So, let's do the math here. The wages of sin is eternal death. We have all sinned, thus we all deserve our wages of destruction (Mt. 10:28; 2 Thess. 1:7-8). That is fairness according to God's holiness.

Trust me, we do not want our salvation to be judged fairly by God. If so, that is nothing but bad news. This would be nothing but doom and condemnation.

Sin cannot just go overlooked since God is a holy God. God's holiness won't allow God to ignore sin. Sin has to be dealt with and this is where God's wrath comes into play.

God's wrath is found all throughout the Old and New Testaments.[32] His wrath must be poured out and sin must be accounted for since God is holy.

So, here is the dilemma in which we find ourselves. Since we have all sinned, we find ourselves separated from God and His grace. The wages of our sin is death (Rom. 6:23).

From this perspective, all hope seems to be lost. It appears we need to pack our bags and go home because there is nothing we can do, in and of ourselves, when we truly understand God's holiness. However, thankfully that is not where the story ends!

You see, for years, I had been preaching what I thought was the gospel. I was preaching my own gospel and not the true gospel that sets men free. The word gospel simply means "good news."[33]

The good news is that we can be saved from our sins (Jn. 1:29)! As Christians, we have been saved through, and by, Jesus Christ (Rom. 5:6-11; 8:31-39). This is the good news (1 Cor. 15:1-4). We

---

[32] Ezek. 7:8-9; Nahum 1:2, 6; Rom. 1:18; Heb. 10:26-31; Rev. 6:16-17; Isa. 63:2-6; Rev. 14:19-20; 2 Thess. 1:7-9
[33] www.biblehub.com/greek/2098.htm, 2098. "Euaggelion"

can be reconciled back to God (2 Cor. 5:12-21). The way I once preached and the way some Christians teach, you would think the gospel is a message of condemnation instead of salvation. But listen to the words of Jesus:

> For God did not send his Son into the world to condemn the world, but to save the world through him. (Jn. 3:17).

While God is holy, holiness is not the only part of God's nature. God is also love (1 Jn. 4:8). This is one of the defining characteristics of God's nature.

Love is what makes Christianity so different than other religions (1 Jn. 3:1). God doesn't want to see anyone die or perish; He wants all to be saved. Notice the following verses:

> For I take no pleasure in the death of anyone, declares the Sovereign Lord... (Ezek. 18:32).

> This is good, and pleases God our Savior, who wants all people to be saved and to come to a knowledge of the truth. (1 Tim. 2:3-4).

> The Lord is not slow in keeping his promise, as some understand slowness. Instead he is patient with you, not wanting anyone to perish, but everyone to come to repentance. (2 Pet. 3:9).

God wants us to be saved and went to great lengths to show us His love. How did God accomplish this? I would find that God's love and God's holiness were harmonized in such a way where the holiness of God was appeased, yet the love of God was fulfilled. In the next chapter, I will talk about how God accomplished this plan.

CHAPTER 38
THE GOSPEL

Since God knew sin would enter the world before creation, He already had a plan that would account for sin when we could not (1 Pet. 1:18-21; Eph. 1:3-6). This plan is so great. This plan is so eloquent. Truly, only a perfect God could have created such a divine plan.

This plan had to include God's holiness and wrath being appeased since God can't just turn off His holiness like a light switch. On the other hand, God can't just turn off His love like a light switch, either. Therefore, this plan had to include God's love being outpoured, too.

God, who is all-knowing,[34] knew mankind would sin before He even created us (1 Pet. 1:18-21; Eph. 1:4). Since God knew we would sin, some have asked why He created us? The reason is because God loves us. Even before we were created, He loved us.[35]

Consider if you have children, you knew beforehand they would disobey, get hurt, have their heart broken, and sin; therefore, why did you choose to have children knowing all of this? You did it because you desired the relationship and wanted them to have life. The same is true with God.

God created us with choice.[36] God didn't create us as lifeless robots. He wanted to give us freedom to choose Him. He wants us to

---

[34] Isa. 46:9-10; Mt. 10:30; Psa. 139:1-4; Prov. 15:3
[35] Psa. 139:13-18; 1 Jn. 4:9-11; Jn. 17:3
[36] Josh. 24:15; 1 Kgs. 18:21; Rev. 22:17; Deut. 30:19; Prov. 3:31; Ja. 4:17; Jn. 6:60-68; Gen. 2:16-17; 1 Cor. 2:6-9

choose and desire Him as He desires us. God loved us first so we could choose to love Him. Paul said:

> You see, at just the right time, when we were still powerless, Christ died for the ungodly. Very rarely will anyone die for a righteous person, though for a good person someone might possibly dare to die. But God demonstrates his own love for us in this: While we were still sinners, Christ died for us. (Rom. 5:6-8).

As humans, we are weak and feeble since we are not God. As a creation, we will never be like our Creator. God could have chosen to create us without choice. However, real relationship always requires a choice. God wants us to want Him. Love is not love if it is forced. God chose us with the hope we would choose Him (1 Jn. 4:7-16).

Therefore, here is the real and true gospel: God sent His son, Jesus, into the world to be a sinless sacrifice for our sins, to die, and to overcome death through the resurrection (Jn. 3:16). He became our substitute by becoming a human and taking on the wrath and penalty we deserve (Phil. 2:5-8). Consider the following verses:

> God made him who had no sin to be sin for us, so that in him we might become the righteousness of God. (2 Cor. 5:21).

> Christ redeemed us from the curse of the law by becoming a curse for us. (Gal. 3:13).

> He himself bore our sins in his body on the cross, so that we might die to sins and live for righteousness; by his wounds you have been healed. (1 Pet. 2:24).

> For Christ also suffered once for sins, the righteous for the unrighteous, to bring you to God. He was put to death in the body but made alive in the Spirit. (1 Pet. 3:18).

The Bible teaches that Jesus became the "propitiation" for our sins (1 Jn. 2:2). We don't really use the term propitiation today, so it is important that we understand what the term means. To make a propitiation means to make an atoning sacrifice in order to appease an angry party.³⁷ Because God is holy, we incur God's anger and wrath since we are sinners.

In order for that wrath to be appeased, a blood sacrifice had to be offered on our behalf (Heb. 9:22). Therefore, a sinless sacrifice is the only thing that could atone for our sins and appease God's holy wrath (Heb. 4:15; Lk.23:15). Consider the following verses:

> Therefore, when Christ came into the world, he said: 'Sacrifice and offering you did not desire, but a body you prepared for me; with burnt offerings and sin offerings you were not pleased. Then I said, 'Here I am—it is written about me in the scroll—I have come to do your will, my God. (Heb. 10:5-7).

> Yet it was the Lord's will to crush him and cause him to suffer, and though the Lord makes his life an offering for sin. (Isa. 53:10).

Only a perfect and sinless sacrifice could atone for our sins. Jesus, who is God the Son, came to earth and became man in order to do what we could not (Jn. 1:1-4, 14). He emptied Himself of His privileges and was forsaken by God the Father and died on the cross in order to become our substitute.³⁸ The Bible says:

> For this reason he had to be made like them, fully human in every way, in order that he might become a merciful and faithful high priest in service to God, and that he might make atonement for the sins of the people. (Heb. 2:17).

> About three in the afternoon Jesus cried out in a loud voice, "Eli, Eli, lema sabachthani?" (which means 'My God, my God, why have you forsaken me? (Mt. 27:46).

> When you were dead in your sins and in the uncircumcision of your flesh, God made you alive with Christ. He forgave us all our sins, having canceled the charge of our legal indebtedness, which

---

[37] https://biblehub.com/greek/2434.htm, 2434. "Hilasmos."
[38] Phil. 2:6-8; Mt. 27:46; Heb. 5:7-9; Mt. 26:36-44; Mt. 27:1-56; Mk. 15:1-41; Lk. 23:1-49; Jn. 19:1-37

stood against us and condemned us; he has taken it away, nailing it to the cross. (Col. 2:13-14).

Paul says that the good news is that Jesus came to this earth, He died for our sins, He was buried, and He was resurrected (1 Cor. 15:1-4). This is truly the gospel. This is the good news!

While our wages of sin is death, Jesus paid that penalty for us and has offered us the gift of eternal life (Rom. 6:23). Jesus became our substitute and there is no substitute for the substitute. The cross is where God's holiness and God's love found true harmony.

As I said before, I had always known these facts. Yet, it wasn't what defined my Christianity. What should define our Christian living and teaching is Christ and Him crucified for our sins (1 Cor. 2:2). Yet, I had turned the gospel into nothing but a few frivolous issues that had nothing to do with Jesus' death, burial, and resurrection.

This whole time I had been trying to earn God's favor by my own works. For once, I finally understood what the gospel was all about and it made perfect sense. This was such a different perspective from what I had considered in the past. The facts were no longer *just* facts. I now began to understand the depth of the gospel.

CHAPTER 39
IS HEAVEN REALLY THAT SMALL?

As the gospel was unfolding in front of my face, I couldn't help but see the love God has for His creation. God's desire is that all be saved as discussed in the last chapter. God went to such great lengths to ensure mankind could be saved that it made me wonder why only a few people would end up in heaven. I had always believed that heaven must be small.

This ideology of a "small heaven" had always made it easy to condemn other people. After all, if only "few" people will make it to heaven, then most people are going to hell.

At one church where I preached, there was a man who said that if the church grows too much, he will get concerned since only a few people are going to heaven. He said the smaller the church, the more faithful it is! Does this belief fit within the idea of the gospel?

I used to believe that Christianity only consisted of a few faithful followers. It was for this reason that I not only condemned all other church affiliations, but I also condemned many within my own church affiliation.

I had convinced myself that I was one of the few faithful Christians and everyone else was lost. I had acquired this belief from misunderstanding a popular passage. In Mt. 7:14, Jesus said:

> But small is the gate and narrow the road that leads to life, and only a few find it. (Mt. 7:14).

I used this verse in many sermons. It is oftentimes preached to instill fear in listeners, reminding them that only few are going to end up going to heaven. I would also remind my audience that when God says few, He means few.[39] There can be no doubt based upon these passages that only few are going to heaven, but how "few" is few in Mt. 7:14? What exactly did Jesus mean by this?

Either Jesus meant "few" without qualification or Jesus meant "few" comparatively. Based upon the context of Scripture, there can be no doubt that Jesus was speaking comparatively. How can we know this?

We can know this because of the promise that was made to Abraham. The promise made to Abraham was speaking of those who would have faith in Jesus Christ (Gal. 3:14; 4:21-31; Rom. 9:1-13). This promise was anything but small.[40]

The amount of people who will be saved by Jesus is said to be more numerous than the stars in the sky (Gen. 15:5), more numerous than the sand on the seashore (Gen. 22:17), and more numerous than the dust on the earth (Gen. 28:14).

Some argue that this promise to Abraham was only in reference to physical Israel and has nothing to do with Christians. However, Paul makes his point abundantly clear that the promise made to Abraham was in reference to those who ultimately would be followers of Christ. Notice the following verses:

> Now you, brothers and sisters, like Isaac, are children of promise. (Gal. 4:28).

> If you belong to Christ, then you are Abraham's seed, and heirs according to the promise. (Gal. 3:29).

> And you are heirs of the prophets and of the covenant God made with your fathers. He said to Abraham, 'Through your offspring all peoples on earth will be blessed.' (Acts 3:25).

---

[39] 1 Pet. 3:20; Rev.3:4
[40] Acts 3:15-26; Gal. 3:14; 4:21-31; Rom. 9:1-13

Unfortunately, like myself, many well-intended Christians have misused and abused Mt. 7:13-14 to teach that few means just a handful of people. Thus, like the man I once met, they have concluded that if they are smaller and more exclusive, they must be more righteous.

This is absolutely false and contradicts the promise made to Abraham 430 years before the Old Covenant of Moses (Gal. 3:15-25). When Jesus spoke of only a few going to heaven, He was speaking comparatively. That is, He was saying few compared to the majority.

Consider that in 2012, a poll was taken that shows only 33 percent of the world's population claim any form of Christianity.[41] Even if we were to assume that all 33 percent were faithful followers of Jesus, this would still be considered few compared to the majority of nonbelievers.[42]

Either way you slice it, the amount of people saved will be as numerous as the stars in the sky, the dust on the earth, and the sand on the seashore.

I understood just how wide-reaching the spiritual kingdom is when I truly considered the whole purpose of Jesus coming to earth. I felt like I was studying the Bible for the first time. I stripped away all of the dogmas and traditions of men and understood the gospel in its true simplistic form (2 Cor. 11:30).

I had been so consumed with myself and making sure I was "perfect," that I didn't even notice my true need for a Savior. It was here that I started to see that there is no law system that can save me.

---

[41] https://www.washingtontimes.com/blog/watercooler/2012/dec/23/84-percent-world-population-has-faith-third-are-ch/

[42] It is also possible that, when considering the historical context of Matthew 7:13-14, Jesus is specifically referencing how only few Jews would be saved and have faith in Jesus, especially during the destruction of Jerusalem (see: 1 Pet. 4:18).

CHAPTER 40

USING THE LAW LAWFULLY

Even when I used to accept the facts of the gospel, I didn't apply them correctly. I had always had no problem saying that we can't access God's grace by works of the Old Testament law.[43]

The truth finally dawned on me when I realized that we can't access God's grace through works of any law system, period (Rom. 3:28; Gal. 2:16; Phil. 3:9).[44]

This whole time I had tried to be saved by my own works. I had tried to *earn* salvation. I had been approaching Christianity through law and didn't even realize it until now.

Those attempting to earn their salvation don't realize that is what they are doing. I had no clue that is what I was doing. I had a misunderstanding of law.

While we can't be justified through any law system, it is equally important to properly understand law. While the apostle Paul was against legalism, he was *for* the law of Christ (Gal. 6:2; 1 Cor. 9:21; Rom. 3:27). Paul said:

We know that the law is good if one uses it properly. (1 Tim. 1:8).

The problem with legalism is not with law itself, but in a misplaced trust and application of the law. Therefore, law in Christianity is not bad. Law is a good thing if we use it correctly and understand its proper place. The problem is that it is very easy to misuse the law and to begin to trust in the law itself for salvation.

---

[43] Rom. 9:31-32; Gal. 5:4; Jn. 1:17
[44] See Chapter 2 of this book for further study.

The Bible uses a juxtaposition of two contradictory terms ("law" and "liberty") when describing the Christian system (Ja. 1:25). While we live by law, we are free in Christ because our "law" is one of faith and not works (Ja. 2:12).

For Christians, this is known as the law of liberty or the law of Christ/God (Rom. 7:25; Gal. 6:2; 1 Cor. 9:21). Paul uses accommodative language and play on words when he speaks of the "law of faith." He said:

> Where, then, is boasting? It is excluded. Because of what law? The law that requires works? No, because of the law that requires faith. For we maintain that a person is justified by faith apart from the works of the law. (Rom. 3:27-28).

Any law in which we are judged by our works will always end in condemnation. It is only through faith that we are justified.

Unfortunately, I had taken the law of faith and had turned it into another works-based system. Yet, that was the very point Paul was refuting. We are not justified based upon the works of the law because there is no way anyone can be justified by their own works.

Not only can we not be justified by the works of any law system, we can't be justified by any works at all, even works of obedience.

We can't access God's grace by human merit through our good works or deeds. We can't gain God's favor through works. The moment we attempt to do so we have fallen back under the condemnation of the works of the law. Consider what Paul said:

> For it is by grace you have been saved, through faith—and this is not from yourselves, it is the gift of God— not by works, so that no one can boast. (Eph. 2:8-9).

> ...he saved us, not because of righteous things we had done, but because of his mercy. He saved us through the washing of rebirth and renewal by the Holy Spirit, whom he poured out on us generously through Jesus Christ our Savior, so that, having been

justified by his grace, we might become heirs having the hope of eternal life. (Titus 3:5-7).

Jesus came to fulfill the Old Covenant and establish the New Covenant (Heb. 9:15-17; Heb. 10:9-10). I came to the realization that when Jesus fulfilled the Old Law (Lk. 24:44), He didn't take one law system away in order to bring a different or more difficult law system.

Man couldn't be justified by the Old Testament law (which has been falsely presumed by some as an "easier" law where God's grace covered more and where God was more tolerant).

Therefore, on what basis does anyone believe they could be justified by a "New Testament law system" (which has been falsely presumed by some to be a "more difficult" law where God's grace doesn't cover as much and He is less tolerant toward believers)? This doesn't even make sense.

Jesus came to show mankind that a law system can't save us! This was the point that I had missed all of those years. He came to take away a law system. In Matthew 5:20, Jesus said:

> For I tell you that unless your righteousness surpasses that of the Pharisees and the teachers of the law, you will certainly not enter the kingdom of heaven. (Mt. 5:20).

I once concluded that Jesus brought a "more difficult" law and we have to be even more obedient to the "new law" than the Pharisees were to the "old law." However, when considering the context, Jesus had something completely different in mind.

Jesus' whole point is that righteousness can't come through law. The scribes and Pharisee's righteousness was a righteousness they attempted to gain through their obedience to the law (Lk. 18:9-14). They felt that they were righteous because of their works (Mt. 23). However, no matter how "good" one may be, one can never be justified by law. Yet, many scribes and Pharisees believed they were justified by their law keeping.

They felt they had lived up to the demands of the law by keeping the law. However, Jesus explains that everyone is guilty of breaking the law, even those "righteous" scribes and Pharisees (Ja. 2:10).

You see, even though someone may have never murdered or committed adultery, Jesus explains that they were still law breakers because they had committed hateful and lustful thoughts (Mt. 5:20-30). Thus, they were condemned by the law (Ja. 2:10).

Who can say that they have never had a hateful or lustful thought? No one can. Jesus' point is simple: Everyone is guilty of law breaking (Rom. 3:10). Jesus was not raising the standard of law or morality in Mt. 5 because wrong thoughts have always been sinful.[45]

Jesus was making the undeniable point that no one can live up to the standards of law. Only Jesus was able to do that (Heb. 4:15).

The scribes and Pharisees were masters at taking parts of the law that they were good at and elevating those parts of the law to the exclusion of others (Mt. 23:23).

In doing so they found self-righteousness, believing that they could save themselves through the law since they were keeping parts of the law that they had been able to corner, creating their own standard of righteousness (Rom. 10:3).

Instead of realizing that they needed a Savior since they couldn't keep the law perfectly, they had deceived themselves into believing they were righteous because of their law keeping. In Mt. 5, Jesus was demonstrating that no matter how "good" one may be, one can never be guilt-free of God's law. All accountable humans are guilty of law breaking.

---

[45] Prov. 15:26; Isa. 59:7; Jer. 4:14; Prov. 6:25; Ex. 20:17; Job 31:1; Lev. 19:17-18; Ex. 23:4-5; Prov. 25:1

We cannot rely upon our own obedience to the law to save us (Rom. 3:23; 6:23). The righteousness that comes from the law cannot save us (Gal. 2:21). Jesus came to fulfill the law (Mt. 5:17).

He came to take away the sins and the curse that the law brings (2 Cor. 5:21; Gal. 3:10-14; 1 Pet. 2:24). There was not, and is not, any law system by which humans can be justified (Gal. 3:21).

If we want to be justified and righteous in the sight of God, our righteousness must exceed the righteousness of the scribes and Pharisees. Our righteousness can't come through law if we want to go to heaven; our righteousness must be different. The only way to exceed their righteousness is by having a righteousness that is apart from the law (Rom. 3:21).

Our righteousness must come through Jesus and be in Jesus (Rom. 3:21-4:25; Gal. 2:17-3:25; Phil. 3:9). No matter how hard one tries to follow God, he or she will always fall short - always!

This is why Jesus came to fulfill the law. He didn't come to take one law system out of the way only to replace it with another. He came to show us that no law system can save mankind!

If our righteousness is going to exceed the righteousness of the scribes and Pharisees, then we must understand that righteousness doesn't come through the law - any law (Rom. 7:13-25). Our righteousness must come through faith in Jesus Christ.

Faith in Jesus Christ is the righteousness that exceeds the righteousness of the scribes and Pharisees. Instead of living in freedom, many Christians have made the New Testament just a different "yoke of bondage" instead of a "law of liberty" (Ja. 1:25).

This whole time, I had been trying to access God's grace through my own system. I was relying on my own works of obedience to ensure me a spot in heaven. I had completely missed the whole concept of God, His grace, and the gospel of Jesus Christ.

In the next chapter, I would like to share a story that demonstrates how there is no way that we can do enough to deserve heaven.

CHAPTER 41
NOT ENOUGH POINTS

When I was re-examining my whole approach to God, I came across a story and it really hit home with me. I had unintentionally been approaching Christianity as if it were a points system.

I felt that if I did enough right, then I would go to heaven. If I didn't do enough right (or if I did enough things wrong), I would go to hell. It reminds me of the following fictional story:

> Three active, dedicated, hard-working Christians had just passed away. As the first two men approached the heavenly gate, they noticed a sign posted which read, "ENTRANCE REQUIREMENT: 1,000 POINTS."

> The first man acted as if 1,000 points was nothing. The second man looked a bit worried. They both walked up to the angel guarding the gate. The first man smiled at the angel and said, "1,000 points? Is that all?" The second man nervously said to the angel, "That requirement seems pretty high. Do you think I could possibly have accumulated that many points?" The angel kindly replied, "Well, why don't you both tell me what you have done, and I will tell you how many points you have earned."

> "Let me start!" the first man said enthusiastically. "Let me tell you everything I did. I was a baptized believer in Christ for 32 years; I taught a Sunday school class for over 12 years; I was a youth chaperone whenever they needed me; and I was a song leader at our church!" "That's wonderful!" said the angel. "Now, let me check my book here. Um..., well that is interesting" the angel said. "None of those things are worth any points."

> The man suddenly became very angry, but he went on with his list of Christian accomplishments. "Well, I gave 10 percent of all my

income, and sometimes even more. I also served as a deacon and elder at my church while I was on earth. I also served on the finance committee and the building committee. I attended every work day at church. I mowed the grass and did repairs. At every fellowship supper I helped set up the chairs and tables and then stayed late and helped take them down."

He looked expectantly at the angel, who smiled sympathetically and answered politely, "That sounds great! Let me see...um...that's odd" the angel said. "That also shows up as zero points."

The man looked as if he were about to go into shock. He spoke rapidly with a sense of desperation: "I invited a lot of people to church and often went visiting with the preacher. I won quite a few people to Christ. I supported the camp program and I even went on a mission trip to India every year. And I never cheated on my income tax!"

The angel tried to speak encouragingly as he said, "That's quite a record of good works! But that's still not worth anything."

The angel looked at the second man and said, "Would you like to try now?" The second man looked down at the ground and said, "I don't even have half as many works as this man. In fact, I just became a Christian two years before I died. If he can't get into heaven, then there is no way I have enough points."

Both of these poor men's faces sagged with futility and their shoulders dropped as they seemed resigned to their fate. "We may as well give up," they mourned. "We can never be good enough to get into Heaven. In fact, it seems impossible for us, or anybody else, to get in there based upon what we did or didn't do."

In the distance, the first two men could see the third man running toward them with a big smile on his face. "You're at the wrong entrance!" he yelled as he pointed his finger at a different entrance. The two men looked up and saw on the other entrance a big sign which read, "ADMISSION: FREE (PAID FOR BY THE GRACE OF GOD)."

"What?" the other two men said. "You mean, we can go to heaven?" "Yes, it has already been paid for. You were just at the wrong entrance." With smiles now on all three of their faces, they walked into heaven and began enjoying their eternal life, all paid for by the grace of God.[46]

When I think about this story, I think about how I used to view salvation as a similar points-based system, although I never would have believed I was trying to earn my way to heaven. In fact, I would have vehemently denied such!

Yet, in actuality, I was trying to "tally my points" hoping I would have enough to be accepted by God. I would learn that there was only one way that I could access God's grace and it wasn't going to be through works.

---

[46] I originally read this story in *Set Free: What the Bible Says About Grace*. Cottrell, 2009. pp. 45-46. There are various versions of this story and I have taken the liberty to make adaptations to the story.

CHAPTER 42
ACCESSING GOD'S GRACE

Everyone who has been saved, is being saved, or will ever be saved will only be saved because of the grace of God who made the atoning sacrifice of Jesus possible (1 Cor. 15:10).

Jesus died on the cross for everyone (Jn. 3:16). The gift is available to all (1 Jn. 2:2). Salvation is a free gift (Rom. 6:23). It is a gift we cannot earn in the least bit (Lk. 17:10).

As humans, God created us with choice to either accept the free gift of salvation and be saved or reject the free gift of salvation and be lost (Acts 13:46); it is our choice (Acts 7:51).

God has given us the ability to realize our own sinfulness and shortcomings as well as the ability to choose to access God's grace and accept His gift if we want to be saved (Rom. 10:11, 13). When writing to the Christians in Thessalonica, Paul said:

> For God did not appoint us to suffer wrath but to receive salvation through our Lord Jesus Christ. (1 Thess. 5:9).

The word translated "receive" here is sometimes translated as "obtain" or "possess." We must choose to receive salvation. God is not going to force it upon us. In reference to Jesus, John said:

> He came to that which was his own, but his own did not receive him. Yet to all who did receive him, to those who believed in his name, he gave the right to become children of God. (Jn. 1:11-12).

The Bible says that the grace of God has appeared to all mankind (Titus 2:11). Jesus died for all. While God's grace is freely available to anyone, not everyone is going to be saved because we must accept God's free gift of grace. We must access God's grace. Just like any gift, it must be accepted.

The crucial question at this point then becomes, "How do we access God's grace?" I was surprised to find that the Bible teaches that we access God's grace through faith apart from any of our works. Notice the following verses:

> For we maintain that a person is justified by faith apart from the works of the law. (Rom. 3:28).

> ... If by grace, then it cannot be based on works; if it were, grace would no longer be grace. (Rom. 11:6).

> However, to the one who does not work but trusts God who justifies the ungodly, their faith is credited as righteousness. (Rom. 4:5).

> Therefore, since we have been justified through faith, we have peace with God through our Lord Jesus Christ. (Rom. 5:1).

> Know that a person is not justified by the works of the law, but by faith in Jesus Christ. So we, too, have put our faith in Christ Jesus that we may be justified by faith in Christ and not by the works of the law, because by the works of the law no one will be justified. (Gal. 2:16).

> Be found in him, not having a righteousness of my own that comes from the law, but that which is through faith in Christ—the righteousness that comes from God on the basis of faith. (Phil. 3:9).

> The people of Israel, who pursued the law as the way of righteousness, have not attained their goal. Why not? Because they pursued it not by faith but as if it were by works. They stumbled over the stumbling stone. (Rom. 9:31-32).

Only sinful mankind could misunderstand such a simple plan. We want to complicate matters and make them much more difficult than they really are. If we say that we access God's grace through anything other than faith, we are adding to God's Word.

The Bible explicitly, unequivocally, and emphatically teaches that we are saved by grace through faith apart from our works.[47]

If faith is the way that we access God's grace, then it is vital that we have a proper understanding of faith. Depending upon one's upbringing and experiences, faith can mean different things to different people. Therefore, we have to understand the biblical understanding of the faith that gives us access to God's grace.

Let's begin with understanding what a biblical faith is *not*. A biblical faith is not physical works (Rom. 3:28; Eph. 2:8-9). Some believe faith and works are one and the same.

They see the word "faith" and interject a whole host of works into the word. However, such is not the case. Even when the crowds asked Jesus what they had to do in order to work the works of God, Jesus turned their works-based question on its head. Notice the following verses:

> Then they asked him, 'What must we do to do the works God requires?' Jesus answered, 'The work of God is this: to believe in the one he has sent.' (Jn. 6:28-29).

Jesus explained that the only way we can access salvation is through faith. While they spoke of the "works" (plural) of man, Jesus spoke of the "work" (singular) of God.[48]

---

[47] Jn. 3:16; Rom. 3:22; Rom. 3:24; Rom. 3:26; Rom. 3:28-30; Rom. 4:3-5; Rom. 4:11; Rom. 4:16; Rom. 5:1; Rom. 5:9; Rom. 9:30; Rom. 9:33; Rom. 10:4; Rom. 10:9-10; Rom. 11:6; Gal. 2:16; Gal. 2:21; Gal. 3:5-6; Gal. 3:8; Gal. 3:14; Gal. 3:22; Gal. 3:24; Eph. 1:3; Eph. 2:8; Phil. 3:9; 1 Tim. 1:16; Acts 16:31; 1 Jn 5:4; Jn 3:15; Jn 20:31; Acts 10:43; Acts 13:39; Jn 8:24
[48] Jn. 4:34; Jn. 5:17; Rom. 14:20

It is easy to try to place the emphasis on our own doing. Instead, Jesus made sure they realized the true work of God is found in what Jesus did/does, not what we do. The crowd's reaction clearly indicates they understood that their response and responsibility to God's work is a genuine faith in Him (Jn. 6:30-40).

Our works are not the same thing as our faith and our faith is not the same thing as our works. Faith and works do have a close relationship which we will be discussing in the next chapter. However, faith and works are separate.

We must also understand that a biblical faith is not simply a mental acceptance. There are many examples of people having a mental acceptance of God or Jesus. Yet, that does not constitute a true faith (Jn. 9:1-24; Jn. 12:42-43). The Bible says that even the demons believe, but that doesn't equate to a biblical faith (Ja. 2:19).

So, what is a "biblical" faith? A biblical faith means to have trust and reliance.[49] A biblical faith isn't just believing "about," but believing "in."[50] Therefore, in order for one to access God's grace, they must have a true faith that trusts in Jesus for salvation.

The Bible teaches that we are justified by grace through Jesus Christ and we access that salvation through a biblical faith, apart from any works. The Bible cannot be clearer on this point. Yet, I still wondered where works fit in to all of this. What was I to make of what the Bible says about works?

---

[49] http://biblehub.com/str/greek/4103.htm. 4103. Pistos.
[50] Gen. 15:6-10; Jn. 12:37-43; Prov. 3:5; Psa. 37:4-6; Psa. 28:7

CHAPTER 43
BUT WHAT ABOUT WORKS?

While I had always believed that we are saved by grace through faith, I had also mistakenly believed that I was justified by my works. It was for this reason that I held to so many faulty beliefs in the past. I was operating from a works-based system and didn't even realize it.

I had a "faith plus works" belief instead of a "grace through faith" belief. For all of those years, my emphasis had been on myself and all that I was doing for Jesus, not on what He had done for me.

Once I studied through all of the passages that teach we access God's grace through faith and not works, I was still unsure about how to harmonize what had been my "go-to" passages about works. For example, Ja. 2:24 says:

> You see that a person is considered righteous by what they do and not by faith alone. (Ja. 2:24).

I had always used this passage to teach that salvation is by faith plus works. However, I could no longer ignore the passages that teach we are saved by faith, apart from any works (Rom. 3:28; Eph. 2:8-9; Titus 3:5-6). So, which is it? Am I saved by God's grace through faith or am I saved by God's grace through faith plus works?

Some have chalked this up to a contradiction between Paul and James. They argue that Paul taught we are saved by faith apart from works, whereas James taught we are saved by faith plus works.

However, such writings should not be viewed as a contradiction. It is always dangerous to pit one passage against another. In reality, the answer is quite simple.

When we consider the book of James, he is refuting the false belief that faith is just a mental acceptance (Ja. 2:19). A true faith is a trust in Jesus that will produce works. James is not saying that it is the actual works that save us. If we can be justified on the basis of works, then we are no longer under grace. The Bible says:

> And if by grace, then it cannot be based on works; if it were, grace would no longer be grace. (Rom. 11:6).

So, what is James saying? James is teaching that a true faith will always produce works (Ja. 2:14-17). One of the examples James uses is the story of Abraham sacrificing his son Isaac (Gen. 22:1-19; Ja.2:21-23).

Abraham had faith in God to the point where he was willing to sacrifice his son for God. Yet, God stopped him before Abraham went through with the actual act itself (Gen. 22:10-12). Even though Abraham didn't actually sacrifice his son Isaac, he had a faith that was willing and had already completed the action in his heart (Heb. 11:17-19).

If someone doesn't have works proceeding from their faith, then they don't have a true faith (Ja. 2:14, 17, 20, 26). James is emphasizing the point that a genuine faith in Christ will produce works (Ja. 2:20-26).

Belief is not the result of behavior. Rather, behavior is the result of belief. It is for this reason that a true faith must precede any biblical actions such as repentance, confession, baptism, giving, worshipping, helping others, etc. Consider the illustration Jesus used pertaining to the vine and branches. Jesus said:

> I am the true vine, and my Father is the gardener. He cuts off every branch in me that bears no fruit, while every branch that does bear fruit he prunes so that it will be even more fruitful. You

are already clean because of the word I have spoken to you. Remain in me, as I also remain in you. No branch can bear fruit by itself; it must remain in the vine. Neither can you bear fruit unless you remain in me. I am the vine; you are the branches. If you remain in me and I in you, you will bear much fruit; apart from me you can do nothing. If you do not remain in me, you are like a branch that is thrown away and withers; such branches are picked up, thrown into the fire and burned. If you remain in me and my words remain in you, ask whatever you wish, and it will be done for you. This is to my Father's glory, that you bear much fruit, showing yourselves to be my disciples. (Jn. 15:1-8).

We are saved by grace through faith; works are the result and proof of a true faith. This can further be seen in the multiple examples of Jesus healing people based upon their faith in Him.[51] We are saved by grace which we access through faith and demonstrate by works.

However, I still had questions about the passages that teach we will be judged by our works.[52] When I studied these passages, I found they aren't dealing with salvation. The final judgment does not determine salvation (Heb. 9:27). We can know we are saved before the final judgment (1 Jn. 5:13; 1 Jn. 4:17-18). Jesus said:

Very truly I tell you, whoever hears my word and believes him who sent me has eternal life and will not be judged but has crossed over from death to life. (Jn. 5:24).

On earth, there is judgment we will receive from ourselves and others. However, what is the purpose of the final judgment from God and what is being judged? The final judgment determines the degrees of reward for individual believers (Mt. 5:19; 18:4)[53] as well as degrees of punishment for the lost (Mt. 10:15; 11:22-24).[54]

---

[51] Mt. 9:22; Mk. 5:34; Lk. 17:19; Lk. 18:42; Mt. 8:13; 15:28
[52] Rom. 2:6-8; Mt. 16:27; 1 Cor. 3:14; 2 Cor. 5:10; 11:15; 2 Tim. 4:14; 1 Pet. 1:17; Rev. 2:23; 20:12-13
[53] Lk. 19:12-19; Ja. 3:1
[54] Lk. 10:12; 12:47-48; 20:47; Jn. 19:11

Those who have rejected Christ as Lord and Savior will be judged based on their works alone. Since the Bible teaches that no one can be justified by works (Galatians 2:16), they will be condemned and held fully accountable for everything they did in this life.

No amount of good works will be sufficient to atone for sin. All their thoughts, words, and actions will be judged against God's perfect standard and each will receive their just penalty.

On the other hand, the salvation of those who trust in Christ is not based upon works. These individuals have accepted the free gift of eternal life and will have heaven for their eternal home (Rom. 6:23). Their works will be judged to determine the degree of reward that they will receive in heaven. Paul makes this clear when he says:

> If anyone builds on this foundation using gold, silver, costly stones, wood, hay or straw, their work will be shown for what it is, because the Day will bring it to light. It will be revealed with fire, and the fire will test the quality of each person's work. If what has been built survives, the builder will receive a reward. If it is burned up, the builder will suffer loss but yet will be saved—even though only as one escaping through the flames. (1 Cor. 3:12-15).

Does this mean that works don't matter? Does this mean that we shouldn't try to do our best? Does this mean that "anything goes" and we can just live life any way we choose? Of course not! We are created to do good works and maintain good works for God's glory. Remember, a true faith will always result in works.

> For we are God's handiwork, created in Christ Jesus to do good works, which God prepared in advance for us to do. (Eph. 2:10).

> The saying is trustworthy, and I want you to insist on these things, so that those who have believed in God may be careful to devote themselves to good works. These things are excellent and profitable for people. (Titus 3:8).[55]

---

[55] ESV

...let your light shine before others, that they may see your good deeds and glorify your Father in heaven. (Mat. 5:16).

When putting all of this together, I came to the following conclusions:

1. We are saved by God's grace through faith which is demonstrated by our works.

2. A true faith will always produce works.

3. The final judgment is not to determine salvation, but rather to determine degrees of punishment and reward.

4. Non-believers are lost and their final judgment, which is based upon their works, has to do with determining their degree of punishment.

5. Believers are saved and their final judgment, which is based upon their works, has to do with determining their degree of reward.

Now that I understood the gospel system, how would this change things for me? Would this be able to answer my questions? What kind of impact would this have on how I approach the Bible, God, and Christianity?

PART 11: CONNECTING THE DOTS

CHAPTER 44

IN SEARCH OF A PERFECT LOVE

One of the first "dots" I started connecting was the dot of fear. If you recall, I discussed my fear in Chapter 33. Fear pretty much characterized my belief system up until this point.

It is no fun living in a continuous spiritual condition of nervousness and anxiety. Instead of a peace that surpasses all understanding, I had a fear that surpassed all understanding for as long as I could remember (Phil. 4:7).

There is no denying that the Bible is full of verses that speak of fearing God.[56] I had convinced myself that the constant fear I lived in was just part of Christianity. At the same time, I was trying to harmonize other teachings found in the Bible that seemed to contradict my feelings of fear such as the verses I discussed earlier in Chapter 33.

For example, the Bible says that we can know we have eternal life (1 Jn. 5:13). We shouldn't fear the judgment. We should have boldness because a perfect love casts out fear (1 Jn. 4:17-19). There is no condemnation for those in Christ (Rom. 8:1). We shouldn't fear death (Heb. 2:14-15).

Confidence in the judgment? A love with no fear? No worry of any punishment? We can know we are saved? While I knew these verses well, I hadn't experienced them in my life. They were foreign concepts to me.

---

[56] Deut. 10:12; Jer. 5:20; Eccl. 12:13; Psa. 25:12-14; 34:11; 76:4-7; Psa. 89:7; 111:10; Prov. 14:26-27; 19:23; Isa. 8:12-13; Mt. 10:28; Lk. 12:4-5

Factually speaking, I knew Christians shouldn't fear death or the judgment. I knew Christians should have a love that casts out all fear. I knew Christians should be at peace and have joy.

Yet, this seemed to conflict with other teachings. How could I have a love that casts out all fear if I am supposed to be fearing God? How could I know I was saved if I couldn't know everything?

With my new understanding of God and the gospel, I decided to re-examine the concept of fear. In my studies, I started to see that there are different kinds of fear. For a parallel, consider what the Bible has to say about judging. There are some passages that command judging and other passages that condemn judging (Mt. 7:1-5; Jn. 7:24; 1 Cor. 5:12).

There is a righteous judgment we are to use and a hypocritical/condemning judgment we are not to use. Context must dictate what type or kind of judging is under consideration. I found the same is true when the Bible speaks of fear.

There are passages that speak of having fear and passages that speak of not having fear. As is the case with judging, context must dictate what type or kind of fear is under consideration.

We must be careful to make sure that we are not injecting our own understanding of the word fear when reading the Bible. Instead, we must allow the Bible and context to tell us what kind of fear is under consideration.

I concluded that the fear for the unbeliever is different than the fear for the believer. The fear that conveys horror, terror, and punishment is in regard to unbelievers or those who have rejected Christ.[57] The fear for the believer is much different. This fear is better understood as having awe and reverence for God. This idea conveys honor and respect. The writer of Hebrews said:

---

[57] Mt. 10:28-29; Heb. 10:26-31; Lk. 12:5; 2 Thess. 1:7-9

Therefore, since we are receiving a kingdom that cannot be shaken, let us be thankful, and so worship God acceptably with reverence and awe, for our 'God is a consuming fire.' (Heb. 12:28-29).

Instead of a terrified fear, I am to have reverence and awe for God. I had heard this explanation about fear before, but I had never pursued it. I thought that Phil. 2:12 clearly showed that the fear Christians are to have is one of terror. For example, when Paul was writing to the Christians in Philippi, he said:

Therefore, my dear friends, as you have always obeyed—not only in my presence, but now much more in my absence—continue to work out your salvation with fear and trembling. (Phil. 2:12).

It seemed pretty clear to me that the fear we are to have is one of trembling. However, I found that while the phrase "fear and trembling" can denote a terrified and insecure demeanor when speaking of those who reject God (Ezek. 12:17-19; Heb. 10:31), it can also mean having respect and reverence.[58] Let me give you a couple of biblical illustrations to demonstrate this point.

In 2 Cor. 7, Paul is telling the Christians in Corinth about the joy of Titus and how he had been encouraged because of the Christians there. Paul was discussing the great affection between the Christians in Corinth and Titus. It is within this context that Paul speaks of Titus and says:

And his affection for you is all the greater when he remembers that you were all obedient, receiving him with fear and trembling. (2 Cor. 7:15).

Does this verse mean that the Christians at Corinth were absolutely terrified of their good friend, Titus? No. When Titus came, were they "shaking in their boots" in horror? Absolutely not.

---

[58] www.biblehub.com/greek/5401.htm, 5401. "Phobos."

Within context, this phrase means that they had great respect and reverence for Titus. I remember meeting a famous person who I greatly admired. I was so excited about meeting him that I was literally trembling because of my excitement and the respect I had for him.

It is within this context that we are to view God, with the greatest awe and admiration. Another verse where this same understanding is applied is found in the book of Ephesians. Paul said:

> Bondservants, be obedient to those who are your masters according to the flesh, with fear and trembling, in sincerity of heart, as to Christ; not with eyeservice, as men-pleasers, but as bondservants of Christ, doing the will of God from the heart, with goodwill doing service, as to the Lord, and not to men, knowing that whatever good anyone does, he will receive the same from the Lord, whether he is a slave or free. And you, masters, do the same things to them, giving up threatening, knowing that your own Master also is in heaven, and there is no partiality with Him. (Eph. 6:5-9).[59]

The slave owners were told not to threaten their slaves but treat them with respect and without favoritism. It is within this framework that the slaves were told to obey with fear and trembling. This fear and trembling isn't a fear and trembling that comes from threats, horror, or a fearful consequence, but rather of honor and respect.

God doesn't expect, nor does He desire, Christians to have a "fear and trembling" of horror and terror. Any belief dependent upon that kind of fear is not going to last very long.

While non-Christians and those who have willfully rejected God should fear God in this way (Mt. 10:28), Christians shouldn't have this kind of fear since we have placed our faith in God and Jesus

---

[59] NKJV

Christ. God desires Christians to have a "fear and trembling" of reverence and honor, not of horror and anxiety.

Up until this point, I carried a misunderstanding of what kind of fear I was to have. In fact, the fear characterized by horror and terror had paralyzed my faith. I can't tell you how many times I used the phrase "just to be on the safe side."

However, I came to believe through my study of the Scriptures that God has not called us to be safe; God has called us to take risks in His name and for His glory. In reality, when we choose to do nothing, we are still doing something.

Jesus made this abundantly clear when he contrasted faith with fear (Mk. 4:40; 5:36). God has called us to act, not sit still. Paul said:

> For God has not given us a spirit of fear, but of power and of love and of a sound mind. (2 Tim. 1:7).[60]

I now knew that if I made my decisions based upon fear, then I was already approaching the situation in an unbiblical way. I was determined to find that perfect love in Christ. I wanted the perfect love that casts out all my fear.

> This is how love is made complete among us so that we will have confidence on the day of judgment: In this world we are like Jesus. There is no fear in love. But perfect love drives out fear, because fear has to do with punishment. The one who fears is not made perfect in love. (1 Jn. 4:17-18).

However, even though I was connecting the dots, my biggest fear was still the fear of being wrong. Since I had operated off of a works-based system for so many years, I was still terrified of getting something wrong. It would be here that I would connect the next dot.

---

[60] NKJV

CHAPTER 45
CONTRARY TO THE LAW

My fear of being wrong about biblical issues was built upon the presupposition that I had to have all the correct beliefs in order to go to heaven. But what if I didn't have to figure out everything?

What if I could be wrong on some issues and still go to heaven? I don't mean purposely, willfully, or rebelliously wrong. I mean what if being a Christian isn't predicated on getting everything right? These thoughts had never crossed my mind until I came across a very interesting passage.

Years ago, I had a friend of mine bring a story in the Bible to my attention that I was somewhat familiar with, but I had never really done any in-depth study on it.

The passage is found in 2 Chron. 30:1-27 and takes place during Hezekiah's reign. I mentioned Hezekiah earlier in Chapter 26. I would like to go back and revisit Hezekiah and this story. Remember, Hezekiah is known as the restoration king. He had a great resume before God. The Bible says:

> This is what Hezekiah did throughout Judah, doing what was good and right and faithful before the Lord his God. (2 Chron. 31:20).

He cleaned out the pagan altars, idols, and temples (2 Kings 18:4). Hezekiah was passionate for doing the right thing and he was faithful to God.

However, when Hezekiah was re-instituting the Passover, there was a problem. Many of the Jews were not ceremonially cleansed according to the law and they ate the Passover meal contrary to the law. The text says:

> Although most of the many people who came from Ephraim, Manasseh, Issachar and Zebulun had not purified themselves, yet they ate the Passover, contrary to what was written... (2 Chron. 30:18).

This was a big problem according to the law because you have unclean Jews taking the Passover contrary to the law. How do you think Hezekiah handled this situation?

Remember, Hezekiah was a man of the law. He was a man of God and he was all about doing things God's way.

Did he rebuke these unclean Jews for eating the Passover contrary to the law? No. Did he condemn them on the spot? No. Did he accuse them of having wrong motives? No. Instead, he prayed that God would accept them if their hearts were in the right place (2 Chron. 30:18-20).

How did God answer Hezekiah's prayer? From my perspective, I would have imagined God saying something like, "Hezekiah, how dare you try to worship with these sinners? They are guilty of error and you are guilty of fellowshipping them. Now you are condemned, too!"

At best, I might have pictured God saying something like, "Well, Hezekiah, I wish I could pardon them, but I can't because they aren't acting in accordance with the law."

However, neither of these responses is anything close to what God did. Instead, God accepted their worship and He healed the people. The text says:

> And the Lord heard Hezekiah and healed the people. (2 Chron. 30:20).

Were they violating the law? Yes, but they were still accepted by God because they had trust in God and their hearts were in the right place. In fact, they decided to go ahead and add an extra week to the Passover because they were having such a wonderful time praising the Lord (2 Chron. 30:21-25).

This would go down in history as one of the greatest "worship events" the Jews ever had. The text says:

> There was great joy in Jerusalem, for since the days of Solomon son of David king of Israel there had been nothing like this in Jerusalem. The priests and the Levites stood to bless the people, and God heard them, for their prayer reached heaven, his holy dwelling place. (2 Chron. 30:26-27).

Who knew that when uncleansed Jews took the Passover contrary to the law (and for an extra week) it would turn out to be one of the greatest worship events in history?

When I first studied this passage, I was perplexed because it went against everything I had ever believed about God and obedience. I wondered how people could be violating the law, yet still be accepted by God.

They were wrong. They had missed it. They were guilty of violating the law. Yet, they were still accepted by God.

Where was the justice? Where was the judgment? Where was the condemnation? They had violated the law. Then, a thought crossed my mind. Perhaps this is what it looks like to be justified by grace through faith.

Instead of living up to a standard perfectly without any error, it is about having your heart in the right place and trusting in God even if you aren't doing everything correctly.

However, I still had questions. While this story is undeniably clear, what about all of the other stories in Scripture that appear to be quite the opposite of this one?

For example, the stories of Nadab, Abihu, Uzzah, and others were still part of the Bible, too. What was I to make of the other stories? I didn't want to be guilty of picking and choosing what I wanted and what I didn't want. Could I find the answer to the alleged contradiction with which I was faced?

CHAPTER 46
DOES GOD CONTRADICT HIMSELF?

Having a story in which people were violating God's law, yet still being accepted by Him, was a new phenomenon for me. Once I had encountered the story of Hezekiah, I quickly learned, though, that it wasn't the only one of its kind.

For example, I re-examined Lev. 10. Here, we read about Nadab and Abihu, but we also read about Aaron's other two sons, Eleazar and Ithamar. They, too, had violated the law. However, they were not condemned like Nadab and Abihu (Lev. 10:8-16). The text says:

> 'Why didn't you eat the sin offering in the sanctuary area? It is most holy; it was given to you to take away the guilt of the community by making atonement for them before the Lord. Since its blood was not taken into the Holy Place, you should have eaten the goat in the sanctuary area, as I commanded.' Aaron replied to Moses, 'Today they sacrificed their sin offering and their burnt offering before the Lord, but such things as this have happened to me. Would the Lord have been pleased if I had eaten the sin offering today?' When Moses heard this, he was satisfied. (Lev. 10:17-20).

This was very interesting to me. Here we have four brothers and two very different outcomes. All four brothers sinned and violated God's law. Nadab and Abihu were killed on the spot while Eleazar and Ithamar's sin was pardoned.

Even though they failed to keep the law properly, they were still accepted. It appears that God showed judgment to Nadab and Abihu while showing mercy to Eleazar and Ithamar.

Another example is found in the life of King David. David willfully lied, coveted, committed adultery, murdered, and unlawfully took Bathsheba to be his wife. By the way, he did all those things in just one story (2 Sam. 11-12).

While David willfully sinned, he was never given the death penalty he truly deserved. While one could argue that David had legal loopholes and was king, this explanation doesn't answer why God decided to show him mercy instead of judgment.

Furthermore, consider Solomon and all the other kings who were accepted by God, even though they worshipped or allowed worship on the high places (1 Kgs. 3:1-15, v.3).

The high places were regional worship centers dedicated to pagan gods. Instead of worshipping God where He commanded, they would worship at these high places, sometimes even mixing pagan worship with their worship to God (Deut. 12:4-5).

Worshipping at these local shrines often included making sacrifices, burning incense, and holding feasts or festivals that God had condemned.[61]

Kings such as Jehoshaphat (1 Kgs. 22:43), Jehoash (2 Kgs. 12:2-3), and Jotham (2 Kgs. 15:34–35) all worshipped/allowed worship on the high places, yet, they were accepted by God and considered to be righteous kings.

Even though they violated the law and didn't take down the high places, God showed them mercy instead of judgment.

On the flip side, think about the story of Ananias and Sapphira in Acts 5:1-11. They lied about how much they were giving and God struck them dead for their lie.

---

[61] 1 Kgs. 3:2–3; 12:32; 13:1–5; 14:23; 2 Kgs. 17:29; 18:4; 23:13–14; Lev. 26:30

Now, compare this to the lie of Peter (Lk. 22:54-62). Peter denied Jesus three times by lying when asked about his relationship with Jesus. Instead of striking him dead, God spared his life.

Why did God kill Nadab and Abihu, yet spare their brothers? Why did God destroy Uzzah, but allow David to live? Why did God have a man stoned for picking up sticks on the Sabbath while allowing Jewish kings to worship on pagan altars?

Why did God kill Ananias and Sapphira for their lie, yet allow Peter to live through his? These examples could be multiplied over and over. The bottom line is that it appears that God gives mercy while at other times He gives judgment.

What made matters worse to me is that many different groups within Christianity choose an "either/or" approach to these stories. Where I had been taking the "Nadab and Abihu story" approach to God without considering the other side, some churches take the "Hezekiah story" approach to God without considering the other side. This explains why both sides feel like they can point to stories to prove their point. Unfortunately, this method pits Scripture against itself.

Instead, I want to harmonize Scripture. I believe Scripture always complements, not contradicts (2 Tim. 3:16-17). I want to make sure I am using a holistic approach when studying the Scriptures. It is the totality of God's Word that is truth (Psa. 119:160).

It would be unfair and irresponsible of me to take stories like Uzzah, Nadab, and Abihu without considering Hezekiah. And it would be unfair and irresponsible of me to take stories like Hezekiah without considering Uzzah, Nadab, and Abihu.

Are we to pick and choose which stories we want? Should we throw out the Bible altogether because of a perceived contradiction in how God handles His creation? Do we just need to hope we catch

Him on a good day? Is God sometimes merciful and other times judgmental without any rhyme or reason?

I have come to believe that the answer is found in the sovereignty of God. When I say the sovereignty of God, I simply mean that God is all-powerful and all-knowing (Psa. 147:5).

At the same time, God's sovereignty is limited within His nature (Mal. 3:6; Psa. 102:27). God can never act in conflict with His nature.[62] He can't perform any action that would contradict who He is. Therefore, every sovereign decision God makes is limited, dictated, and predicated by His divine nature. With this in mind, the ultimate question for me became, "How is God judging our obedience and disobedience?"

---

[62] Heb. 6:18; Hab. 1:13; 1 Jn. 4:8; Jer. 31:3

CHAPTER 47
LISTEN TO OUR HEARTS

When I started to take a holistic approach toward God and how He views His creation, I was left with the inescapable conclusion that God judges our hearts. This certainly caught me off guard. The idea of God looking at our hearts was actually something at which I used to poke fun.

I used to say that people are using that as an excuse to try to get out of following God. I would hear people talk about how God knows their hearts. I would respond by telling them that God is interested in our actions and our hearts are only as good as our actions. I used to believe that it didn't matter how good your heart was if your actions were wrong.

Yet, with the aforementioned biblical stories in mind, I now realize that God judges our obedience and disobedience based upon our hearts. The Bible teaches that God knows the hearts of men (Jer. 17:10; Jn. 2:24; Mk. 2:8). Consider the following passages:

...would not God have discovered it, since he knows the secrets of the heart? (Psa. 44:21).

...for you alone know every human heart... (1 Kings 8:39).

God doesn't see as man sees. We have limited understanding while God has endless discernment (1 Jn. 3:20; Psa. 139:4). We can never fully understand what lies within a man (1 Cor. 2:11).

God always has a reason why He does what He does and it is always predicated on the heart of the individual (Rom. 11:33; Isa.

55:8-9). God is ultimately looking at the heart. Notice just a few of the passages that teach this:

> ...The LORD does not look at the things people look at. People look at the outward appearance, but the LORD looks at the heart. (1 Sam. 16:7).

> Rejoice in the Lord and be glad, you righteous; sing, all you who are upright in heart! (Psa. 32:11).

> For the eyes of the Lord range throughout the earth to strengthen those whose hearts are fully committed to him... (2 Chron. 16:9).

Even with all of King David's willful sin, he was still considered a man after God's own heart (Acts 13:22; 1 Sam. 2:35; Jer. 3:15). Even though we all fall short, God saves those who have a good heart and have placed their trust in Him.

Sometimes we sin ignorantly and sometimes we even sin willfully. To deny such is to deny truth (1 Jn. 1:10). Our spirit is willing, but our flesh is weak (Mt. 26:41). That is why we must work on our hearts. The Bible says:

> My shield is God Most High, who saves the upright in heart. (Psa. 7:10).

When Jesus was physically on earth, He placed the emphasis on the heart. While the scribes and Pharisees were more concerned about the outward action, Jesus was concerned with what was on the inside (Mt. 23:25-28). Consider the story about Simon the Pharisee and the sinful woman:

> When one of the Pharisees invited Jesus to have dinner with him, he went to the Pharisee's house and reclined at the table. A woman in that town who lived a sinful life learned that Jesus was eating at the Pharisee's house, so she came there with an alabaster jar of perfume. As she stood behind him at his feet weeping, she began to wet his feet with her tears. Then she wiped them with her hair, kissed them and poured perfume on them."

When the Pharisee who had invited him saw this, he said to himself, 'If this man were a prophet, he would know who is touching him and what kind of woman she is—that she is a sinner.' Jesus answered him, 'Simon, I have something to tell you.' 'Tell me, teacher,' he said.

'Two people owed money to a certain moneylender. One owed him five hundred denarii, and the other fifty. Neither of them had the money to pay him back, so he forgave the debts of both. Now which of them will love him more?' Simon replied, 'I suppose the one who had the bigger debt forgiven.' 'You have judged correctly,' Jesus said.

Then he turned toward the woman and said to Simon, 'Do you see this woman? I came into your house. You did not give me any water for my feet, but she wet my feet with her tears and wiped them with her hair. You did not give me a kiss, but this woman, from the time I entered, has not stopped kissing my feet. You did not put oil on my head, but she has poured perfume on my feet. Therefore, I tell you, her many sins have been forgiven—as her great love has shown. But whoever has been forgiven little loves little.' Then Jesus said to her, 'Your sins are forgiven.' The other guests began to say among themselves, 'Who is this who even forgives sins?' Jesus said to the woman, 'Your faith has saved you; go in peace.' (Lk 7:36-50).

We learn in this story what it means to follow Jesus. While Simon, the Pharisee, wanted to condemn the sinful woman, the sinful woman was justified. Why? Because she had kept the righteous list of requirements of the law? No. On the contrary, she failed miserably at keeping the law.

I realized that having our sins forgiven is not predicated upon us getting everything right. Jesus is concerned with the heart. Everyone knew this woman for her sinfulness. Yet, she was accepted by Jesus. While others were concerned with judgment, Jesus showed this woman mercy because of her loving heart and her desire to follow Him.

I would like to parallel that story with a well-known parable told by Jesus which comes from Lk. 10:25-37. This parable is about a good Samaritan. The Samaritans were hated by the Jews. They were considered "half-breeds" who didn't know how to worship properly (Jn. 4:22).

When a man asked Jesus what he had to do in order to inherit eternal life, Jesus told him he had to love his neighbor as himself. The man then asked Jesus who his neighbor was. Jesus responded by telling a parable about a man who was robbed and left for dead.

While a priest and a Levite saw this helpless man in need, they didn't show love and mercy. Instead, it was a Samaritan who stopped and helped the man. Jesus concluded by asking a question about the parable:

> 'Which of these three do you think was a neighbor to the man who fell into the hands of robbers?' The expert in the law replied, 'The one who had mercy on him.' Jesus told him, 'Go and do likewise.' (Lk. 10:36-37).

While the Jewish priest and Levite held high positions, they lacked the proper heart. It was the Samaritan who was justified in the story because he ultimately fulfilled the law by showing mercy and loving his neighbor as himself:

> Let no debt remain outstanding, except the continuing debt to love one another, for whoever loves others has fulfilled the law. The commandments, 'You shall not commit adultery,' 'You shall not murder,' 'You shall not steal,' 'You shall not covet,' and whatever other command there may be, are summed up in this one command: 'Love your neighbor as yourself.' Love does no harm to a neighbor. Therefore love is the fulfillment of the law. (Rom. 13:8-10).

While this Samaritan worshipped contrary to the law and wasn't accepted by the Jews, he was accepted by God. Why? Because he had obeyed all of God's commands and got everything right? No. It was because he fulfilled the law by loving his neighbor as himself.

Whether it was the uncleansed Jews who partook of the Passover contrary to the law, the immoral woman who brought all she had to Jesus, or the Samaritan who didn't know how to worship (but knew how to love his neighbor); they all had one thing in common: They all shared the same kind of heart. Thank God that He looks at the heart! David said:

> My sacrifice, O God, is a broken spirit; a broken and contrite heart you, God, will not despise. (Psa. 51:17).

As we have learned, obedience doesn't always necessitate a good heart and disobedience doesn't always necessitate a bad heart. At the same time, there are those who appear to be obedient and may be obedient, but they lack a proper heart. God doesn't judge us in isolated instances; He looks at our whole heart.

One of the strongest illustrations that helped me understand this point comes from Paul. He said that even if someone were to help the homeless, the poor, and even die for the cause of Christ, but not have love, then it profits them nothing (1 Cor. 13:3). You would think dying for Jesus would be a one-way ticket to heaven. Yet, that is not the case.

Paul said that some may even die for Jesus, but still have a wrong heart. According to 2 Chron. 30, with Hezekiah we see an example of God accepting good hearts with wrong actions. In 1 Cor. 13, we read about God rejecting obedient actions because they were accompanied with bad hearts.

I would also like to point out that just because we aren't going to get everything right doesn't mean we shouldn't strive for perfection. Certainly, we should always be trying to perform the right actions. Yes, doing the right thing is important (2 Tim. 2:5).

However, we need to remember that we constantly fall short and at the end of the day, God is looking at our hearts. Even Paul knew there would never be a point where he would get it all right. Paul said:

Not that I have already obtained all this, or have already arrived at my goal, but I press on to take hold of that for which Christ Jesus took hold of me. Brothers and sisters, I do not consider myself yet to have taken hold of it. But one thing I do: Forgetting what is behind and straining toward what is ahead, I press on toward the goal to win the prize for which God has called me heavenward in Christ Jesus. (Phil. 3:12-14).

None of this should cause anyone to feel justified in continuing in willful and rebellious sin (Rom. 6:1-2; Gal. 2:19-21). Rather, it should cause the seeker to be confident because we can "know that we have eternal life" (1 Jn. 5:13).

With all of these things in mind, I still wondered about those verses that I had used in the past about God's grace not covering ignorance. How was I to harmonize those verses with the clear times God did overlook ignorance? Maybe God used to be more forgiving and graceful, but now He isn't anymore? What was I to make of God, error, ignorance, and grace?

CHAPTER 48
GOD'S GRACE AND MY IGNORANCE

Up until this point, I had taught that if someone is guilty of "error" or sin (even ignorantly), then they are lost if they don't repent. This was something I believed and taught others for years.

I further oversimplified this belief by saying that God couldn't forgive ignorant sin since we must repent of our sins in order to go to heaven.

I would reason that if we have ignorant sin in our lives, we can't repent of it until we know about it. Therefore, if we die with ignorant sin in our lives, we die with unrepented sin in our lives. Thus, we die in a lost state.

There were several verses I once used to try to say that God demands perfect obedience and that we can't be wrong (whether willfully or ignorantly) and still go to heaven unless we first repent of every sin. One of the verses I used was Acts 17:30. The text says:

> In the past God overlooked such ignorance, but now he commands
> all people everywhere to repent.

I used to use this verse to teach that while God may have looked at the heart under the Old Testament, today God overlooks no ignorance and we must be right on absolutely everything to go to heaven. Needless to say, I was gravely mistaken as to the meaning of this verse.

Acts 17:30 does not teach that God requires Christians to have perfect obedience while tolerating zero ignorance. This verse isn't even about Christians. Paul was speaking to pagans in Acts 17:30 while referencing the pagans during the time of the Old Testament. Under the Old Law, even though Gentiles could convert to Judaism (Isa. 56:1-12), God allowed the pagan Gentiles to live by the law written in their hearts (Rom. 2:12-16). God allowed this during the Old Testament since the law was only given to the Jews.

Acts 17:30 certainly isn't about the Jews being ignorant because they were never ignorant. The law was given to them. While they messed it up miserably, they were not ignorant of the law.

The whole point of Rom. 2-3 is to show that the Jews had the advantage over the Gentile's because they had full access to God from the beginning, whereas God overlooked the Gentile's ignorance during that time. Paul said:

> What advantage, then, is there in being a Jew, or what value is there in circumcision? Much in every way! First of all, the Jews have been entrusted with the very words of God. (Rom. 3:1-2).

It was the pagan Gentiles who were ignorant. They didn't have the law of Moses; they only had the law written in their hearts. It was the ignorance of the pagan Gentiles that God overlooked during that time. Paul said:

> Indeed, when Gentiles, who do not have the law, do by nature things required by the law, they are a law for themselves, even though they do not have the law. They show that the requirements of the law are written on their hearts, their consciences also bearing witness, and their thoughts sometimes accusing them and at other times even defending them. (Rom. 2:14-15).

In Acts 17, Paul made the point that Jesus had come to the earth to break down the middle wall of separation between the Jew and the Gentile (Mt. 28:19-20; Col. 1:23). Paul was letting them know that the gospel of Jesus Christ is for all (Rom. 1:16). No longer can man access God except through Jesus Christ (Jn. 14:6; Acts 4:12).

Therefore, the reference in Acts 17:30 about ignorance being overlooked is about the non-believing pagan Gentiles who lived before the New Covenant. Acts 17:30 has nothing to do with the Christian and ignorance. Rather, it has to do with those living under the New Law who never placed their faith in Jesus.

I once heard a preacher use this verse to say that if you were driving down the road and said a curse word right before you died in a car wreck, God's grace couldn't cover you because you didn't have an opportunity to repent of saying that bad word.

Acts 17:30 does not teach that one has to be "sinlessly perfect" the moment he or she dies in order to go to heaven. The truth of the matter is that we will all die as imperfect humans falling short of God's will.

Another passage that is sometimes misused comes from a parable in Lk. 12:35-48. At the end of the parable, Jesus said:

> The servant who knows the master's will and does not get ready or does not do what the master wants will be beaten with many blows. But the one who does not know and does things deserving punishment will be beaten with few blows. From everyone who has been given much, much will be demanded; and from the one who has been entrusted with much, much more will be asked. (Lk. 12:47-48).

Similar to Acts 17:30, Lk. 12:47-48 is speaking of ignorance in regard to those who have rejected Jesus as the Messiah. It isn't speaking of believers who may have a misunderstanding on an issue.

Jesus is speaking about those who don't have faith in Him (Lk. 12:48). Jesus was teaching this parable to those (specifically the Jews) who would deny Him (Lk. 12:49-53). Many Jews would reject Jesus and continue to try to be saved through the law of Moses (Rom. 10:1-3). Therefore, this parable isn't in relation to Christians, but to non-Christians who don't possess a faith in Jesus.

When I started to study and reconsider the passages that talk about ignorance, I realized that these passages are speaking about those outside of Jesus Christ. They are speaking of non-believers, not believers. They address ignorance within the context of those who didn't place their faith in Jesus, not those who did place their faith in Jesus.

These passages teach us that we can only be saved if we come to Jesus in faith (Jn. 14:6). Passages such as these are speaking of those who aren't seeking salvation through Jesus (Acts 4:12). The point Jesus and Paul make is that it doesn't matter if you're a Jew or a Gentile, if you aren't seeking salvation through Jesus, then your ignorance won't be overlooked as a non-believer as it once was under the Old Law.

As I continued to study the idea of grace, mercy, sin, and ignorance, I started to see more clearly how I had mistakenly been viewing God and Christianity. I had not been wrong about just one or two issues; I had been viewing everything through a faulty framework. I had been viewing everything through the lenses of law and this had affected my Christianity on many levels. This is when I knew it was time to make a system change in my Christianity.

PART 12:
THE CHANGE

CHAPTER 49
THE MOST IMPORTANT CHAPTER

If this is your first time opening up the book and you decided to start here because of the chapter title, please do not read this chapter yet. This chapter will only make sense if you have read the other chapters up until this point.

This is the most important chapter in the book because this is when the meaningful change took place for me. This is the "aha moment." I am so excited to share this chapter with you! You have had to endure a lot to get to this chapter, but you have finally made it.

The reason this chapter is the most important is because nothing else in this book matters if you don't understand this chapter. If you don't get what is in this chapter, then you will never be able to overcome legalism. This chapter is that important.

If you have been reading, taking notes, and following along carefully up until this point, then when you apply the things within this chapter, it will absolutely change your life forever.

I am fully convinced that many people have left some elements of legalism but are still trying to figure out many things because they still have the wrong framework.

What I am about to say is very counterintuitive, but it is so important to accept: You can't study your way out of legalism through the framework of legalism. Up until this point in my life, I was still very legalistic without realizing it.

Yes, I had changed on so many levels. Yes, I had kicked many of my legalistic symptoms. However, I was still operating from the same framework I had always used. I was still viewing Scripture through law. I was still viewing Christianity through the lenses of legalism.

This is why you have individuals who are grace-centered toward people, but are still very dogmatic, closed-minded, and inconsistent in their approach toward Scripture.

On the flipside, this is also why you have people who are very open-minded in their approach toward Scripture and biblical issues, but are still very divisive, harsh, and argumentative in their approach toward people. In both scenarios, legalism is still the framework. Do you see it? Is it making sense, yet?

Please, do not miss this point. Even after I changed in so many ways, I still missed this point completely for a couple of years. If you miss this point, then the whole purpose of my book has failed. For years I missed the forest for the trees. I was still very issue-oriented, and I wasn't looking at the bigger picture.

Since I was still infected with legalism at this point in my life, I was continuing to experience problems in my personal study and application. While I was not being legalistic toward people anymore, I still unintentionally approached God and the Bible through the lenses of law.

I was still confused on how to figure out a standard of unity and fellowship. I had experienced changes on biblical issues, but I had not experienced a true system change yet. I had accepted that God looks at the heart, but I was still viewing that concept through law to an extent. Let me explain.

You see, through the framework of law, the story of Hezekiah and Israel doesn't work. Through the framework of law, the story of Eleazar and Ithamar doesn't make sense. Through the framework of law, Jesus couldn't be the Messiah! Are you following this?

The scribes and Pharisees viewed Jesus through the framework of law. This is the very reason they missed Jesus! They had the wrong framework.

They had the knowledge. They even had the wisdom! However, Christianity doesn't make sense within the framework of law, no matter how much Bible knowledge or wisdom you have.

It is like watching a movie with the wrong audio. You see what is there, but you don't really know what is happening. The Jews had been approaching Jesus through law and they missed Him. Jesus said:

> You study the Scriptures diligently because you think that in them you have eternal life. These are the very Scriptures that testify about me. (Jn. 5:39).

We cannot view Christianity through the lenses of law. That doesn't mean that there is no law in Christianity (see Chapter 40). We just need to make sure we don't view Christianity through the lenses of a law system.

Even though I didn't want it to be, my Christianity up until this point had been very ritualistic. I thought what I was doing was true Christianity. I got used to going through the motions.

It reminded me of high school when we had required reading every year. The teacher would ask us if we had read the specific books on the list. Technically speaking, I could honestly say I had "read" the books.

I couldn't have told you what I read, but I knew that I flipped the pages as I quickly skimmed some words so I could say that I did what I was supposed to do.

As silly as it may sound, my Christianity oftentimes felt a lot like required reading. It was more about getting it done than actually doing it. Just like in school, I was more concerned with passing the test and the technicalities than I was knowing my teacher. I found myself having a checklist mentality. I noticed how ritualistic everything in my Christianity had become. Notice the words of Jesus:

> Woe to you, teachers of the law and Pharisees, you hypocrites! You give a tenth of your spices--mint, dill and cumin. But you have neglected the more important matters of the law--justice, mercy and faithfulness. You should have practiced the latter, without neglecting the former. (Mt. 23:23).

Certainly, having rituals are not wrong in and of themselves. In fact, rituals are a good thing, especially if they are biblical. Jesus told the scribes and Pharisees that they should have practiced the latter *without* neglecting the former.

However, just like the scribes and Pharisees, I had allowed my rituals to become my Christianity while ignoring the weightier matters of the law. It is when we begin to allow rituals to take over that we forget what following God is all about.

Do we actually *know* Jesus? The Bible teaches that Christianity must be viewed through the lenses of relationship, not ritual, and grace, not law (Jn. 1:14; Rom. 6:14). Jesus said:

> Now this is eternal life: that they know you, the only true God, and Jesus Christ, whom you have sent. (Jn. 17:3).

The word used here for "know" in this verse is much more than "fact knowledge" (Rom. 1:21). It isn't just knowing about Jesus; it is knowing Jesus Himself. The very definition of this word means, "to know, especially through personal experience (first-hand acquaintance)."[63]

This is the same word used in Luke 1:34 when dealing with intimacy. To know Jesus is a theme that is constantly seen throughout the New Testament (2 Thess. 1:7-9). When John was

---

[63] www.biblehub.com/greek/1097.htm, 1097. Ginóskó.

writing in 1 John, he also spoke of the importance of knowing God and Jesus Christ. He said:

> Dear friends, let us love one another, for love comes from God. Everyone who loves has been born of God and knows God. (1 Jn. 4:7).

> We know also that the Son of God has come and has given us understanding, so that we may know him who is true. And we are in him who is true by being in his Son Jesus Christ. He is the true God and eternal life. (1 Jn. 5:20).

I used to argue that we can't have a personal relationship with Jesus because He isn't physically here. This faulty conclusion, however, misses the spiritual nature of Christianity and the kingdom.

Jesus Christ is currently reigning in His Kingdom of which all Christians share a part (Col. 1:13; Heb. 1:3; Acts 2:29-33). Our relationship with Christ is spiritual. Paul declared a personal relationship with Jesus when He said:

> I have been crucified with Christ and I no longer live, but Christ lives in me. The life I now live in the body, I live by faith in the Son of God, who loved me and gave himself for me. (Gal. 2:20).

The major problem in legalism has always been with people knowing about God, but never knowing Him deeply and intimately. We can't know Jesus through law; we can only truly know Him through relationship.

Let me illustrate this point. I want you to think of men like Sam Walton, the founder of Wal-Mart. Consider his employees. How many employees of Wal-Mart do you think ever met Mr. Walton when he lived, much less had a personal relationship with him? Most showed up to work never really knowing him.

Sure, they heard of Mr. Walton and knew his demands, but didn't really know him. They worked for him expecting something in return. If they met his demands, they would get paid for their work. If they didn't meet his demands, they would lose their job.

Unfortunately, I once viewed Christianity in a similar light. If I just showed up to get the job done and if I did my job correctly, then I would receive my reward when I died because I put my hours in. I never knew Jesus, but I just knew that He was "the guy" for whom I worked in order to "gain" heaven. I now realize that Christianity is all about our relationship with Christ.

This was when things finally changed for me. This was when the system change took place. You can change your approach toward others and you can change your position on a host of biblical issues, but until you view Christianity through the framework of a relationship with Jesus, you will never experience Christian living the way Jesus intended.

We are now under a relationship/grace system, not a ritual/law system.[64] Yes, there are still laws (1 Jn. 3:4; Rom. 4:15), but they are not viewed in light of a law system. They are viewed through relationship (Rom. 6:14). In this section, for the next several chapters, we will be exploring this concept in depth.

---

[64] 2 Cor. 3:1-18; Ja. 2:9-13; Jn. 17:3

CHAPTER 50
THE WILL OF GOD: KNOWING JESUS

When I viewed Christianity through the framework of law, I would often quote Mt. 7:21-23 when condemning others. Here, Jesus says:

> Not everyone who says to me, 'Lord, Lord,' will enter the kingdom of heaven, but only the one who does the will of my Father who is in heaven. Many will say to me on that day, 'Lord, Lord, did we not prophesy in your name and in your name drive out demons and in your name perform many miracles?' Then I will tell them plainly, 'I never knew you. Away from me, you evildoers!'

I must have quoted Mt. 7:21-23 several hundred times before finally understanding the context. In Mt. 7:21, Jesus tells us that we must do the will of God if we want to go to heaven.

Ironically, I had abused this passage so many times to teach the exact opposite of what Jesus was teaching. I used to say that Mt. 7:21-23 meant we must *perfectly* understand and execute God's commands. Otherwise, we haven't done God's will. I was actually using this text to teach a works/law-based salvation instead of a faith/relationship-based salvation.

Jesus' point in this context is that there will be many who do all kinds of rituals and works in His name, but don't really *know* Him. They never had a relationship with Him. They were relying on their own works instead of the grace of God to save them.

Many will come to Jesus on the day of judgment to bring them their "list" of works and good deeds. They will try to be justified based upon what they did. Instead of relationship, they will rely upon ritual and works. Jesus was teaching that Christianity is not a ritualistic, works-based system founded upon how many good works we can bring to God.

In Mt. 7:22-23, Jesus was teaching us that we can't trust in our works. Rather, we must trust and know Him. Our works are worth nothing to Jesus in the way of earning salvation. Many will try to bring their "points" to Jesus, but it will only be those who *know* Jesus who will enter heaven.

The very gospel that Jesus came to preach is the exact opposite of the mentality that I once had. We are to have a fellowship with Jesus, not just an association (1 Jn. 1:3; 1 Cor. 1:9).

We are to know Jesus and you can only know someone if you have a relationship with them. If we don't have a relationship with Jesus, then how can we claim we know Him? And if we claim we know Him, then how can we deny a relationship with Him?

Some have taken this idea to mean that we can do whatever we want to do. However, such is not the case. Such an erroneous position can be easily refuted. Paul dealt with the same misunderstanding of law and grace when he said:

> What then? Shall we sin because we are not under the law but under grace? By no means! (Rom. 6:15).

Law certainly exists today. As we have already established, the very definition of sin is to violate law (1 Jn. 3:4). Since we have all sinned, then we have all violated law (Rom. 3:23).

Paul teaches that Christians exist within the works of the law, but we are not judged under the works of the law (Rom. 6:15; Gal. 3:21-22; Rom. 11:6). If we are, then we would all be condemned (Ja. 2:10).

This was extremely hard for Paul's audience to understand, especially for the Jews. In their mind, if they were not under the works of the law, then they could do whatever they wanted. Paul aggressively corrected this mentality. He said:

> ...know that a person is not justified by the works of the law, but by faith in Jesus Christ. So we, too, have put our faith in Christ Jesus that we may be justified by faith in Christ and not by the works of the law, because by the works of the law no one will be justified. But if, in seeking to be justified in Christ, we Jews find ourselves also among the sinners, doesn't that mean that Christ promotes sin? Absolutely not! If I rebuild what I destroyed, then I really would be a lawbreaker. For through the law I died to the law so that I might live for God. I have been crucified with Christ and I no longer live, but Christ lives in me. The life I now live in the body, I live by faith in the Son of God, who loved me and gave himself for me. I do not set aside the grace of God, for if righteousness could be gained through the law, Christ died for nothing! (Gal. 2:16-21).

Viewing Christianity through the framework of relationship isn't a license to sin. On the contrary, it gives us even more reason to love God and be obedient to Him. In the next chapter, I want to delve further into the idea of a relationship and what that actually means according to the Scriptures.

CHAPTER 51
RELATIONAL ILLUSTRATIONS

What does it mean to have a relationship with Jesus? It was very interesting when I studied the biblical concept of "knowing" Jesus. I had never viewed Christianity in that way. This was a whole new perspective.

Aside from the biblical passages that talk about "knowing" Jesus, I now want us to look at the different relational illustrations found in the Bible so we can better understand Jesus and the relationship He desires us to have with Him.

Husband and Wife- The Bible illustrates our relationship to Jesus by paralleling it to a husband and wife couple (Eph. 5:22-32). Notice the words of Paul:

> Wives, submit yourselves to your own husbands as you do to the Lord. For the husband is the head of the wife as Christ is the head of the church, his body, of which he is the Savior. Now as the church submits to Christ, so also wives should submit to their husbands in everything. Husbands, love your wives, just as Christ loved the church and gave himself up for her to make her holy, cleansing her by the washing with water through the word, and to present her to himself as a radiant church, without stain or wrinkle or any other blemish, but holy and blameless. In this same way, husbands ought to love their wives as their own bodies. He who loves his wife loves himself. After all, no one ever hated their own body, but they feed and care for their body, just as Christ does the church— for we are members of his body. 'For this reason a man will leave his father and mother and be united to his wife, and the two will become one flesh.' This is a profound mystery—but I am talking about Christ and the church (Eph. 5:22-32).

Here, the emphasis is put on having a deep, submissive, and sacrificial love just as a husband and wife have for one another. Therefore, how should I view my relationship with Jesus? I should view it like that of a spouse. This also shows us the constant continuation of our relationship with Jesus every day.

Friend – Jesus came to earth to be our friend:

> You are my friends if you do what I command. (Jn. 15:14).

I would often emphasize only the second half of John 15:14 instead of the first half. I would say if you want to be a friend of Jesus, you have to keep all His commandments perfectly.

I would unintentionally misuse this verse as a proof text to show why someone was not really a friend of Jesus if they were doing just one thing incorrectly.

However, perfect law keeping is nowhere in view in the context of John 15:14 (or in the Bible for that matter). Instead, consider the verses surrounding the context that show what command Jesus was emphasizing when he spoke of being our friend:

> A new command I give you: Love one another. As I have loved you, so you must love one another. By this everyone will know that you are my disciples, if you love one another. (Jn. 13:34-35).

> If you really know me, you will know my Father as well. From now on, you do know him and have seen him. (Jn. 14:7).

> My command is this: Love each other as I have loved you. Greater love has no one than this: to lay down one's life for one's friends. You are my friends if you do what I command. I no longer call you servants, because a servant does not know his master's business. Instead, I have called you friends, for everything that I learned from my Father I have made known to you. You did not choose me, but I chose you and appointed you so that you might go and bear fruit—fruit that will last—and so that whatever you ask in my name the Father will give you. This is my command: Love each other. (Jn. 15:12-17).

If we want to be friends with Jesus, we must know Him and love one another as Jesus loves us. The command Jesus spoke of in John 15:14 is love for one another. John writes:

> Whoever claims to love God yet hates a brother or sister is a liar. For whoever does not love their brother and sister, whom they have seen, cannot love God, whom they have not seen. (1 Jn. 4:20).

Jesus always exemplified the type of friendship that we should have with Him and one another. One example of this can be seen when Jesus washed the disciple's feet (Jn. 13:1-17). This is the kind of love Jesus has for us and the kind of love we should have for others. He is not just our friend; He should be our best friend.

Brother – Jesus is said to be our brother.

> He replied to him, 'Who is my mother, and who are my brothers?' Pointing to his disciples, he said, 'Here are my mother and my brothers. For whoever does the will of my Father in heaven is my brother and sister and mother.' (Mt. 12:48-50).

He isn't ashamed to be called our brother (Heb. 2:11). Jesus shows His relationship with us by showing us that He is our brother. We have a sibling relationship with Jesus.

Child – All Christians are part of the family of God. Gal. 4:1-7 says:

> What I am saying is that as long as an heir is underage, he is no different from a slave, although he owns the whole estate. The heir is subject to guardians and trustees until the time set by his father. So also, when we were underage, we were in slavery under the elemental spiritual forces of the world. But when the set time had fully come, God sent his Son, born of a woman, born under the law, to redeem those under the law, that we might receive adoption to sonship. Because you are his sons, God sent the Spirit of his Son into our hearts, the Spirit who calls out, 'Abba, Father.' So you are no longer a slave, but God's child; and since you are his child, God has made you also an heir...'

The Bible describes the relationship with God as a parent-child relationship through Jesus Christ. We are to be obedient to Christ and God the Father as a child would be to their parent, but God is also supportive, forgiving, merciful, and loving just as a good Father would be to their child.

Lord - Jesus is our Lord. It isn't enough to claim a relationship with Jesus when one does not actually have a relationship with Him. Jesus said:

> Why do you call me, 'Lord, Lord,' and do not do what I say? (Lk. 6:46).

Jesus must be the Lord of our lives. While there is a sense that God is seen as our master and we are seen as His servants (Rom. 6:18-20), that is only in light of us belonging to Christ. As far as role, we are no longer a slave but a friend and a part of the family. Notice the following verses:

> I no longer call you servants, because a servant does not know his master's business. Instead, I have called you friends, for everything that I learned from my Father I have made known to you (Jn. 15:15).

> Because you are his sons, God sent the Spirit of his Son into our hearts, the Spirit who calls out, "Abba, Father." So you are no longer a slave, but God's child; and since you are his child, God has made you also an heir (Gal. 4:6-7).

Our approach to Christianity will drastically change when we realize it is about a relationship and not a ritualistic system. It will become transformative instead of merely informative. It won't be just about perfecting our worship assemblies or outward actions. Consider the words of Paul:

> Therefore, I urge you, brothers and sisters, in view of God's mercy, to offer your bodies as a living sacrifice, holy and pleasing to God—this is your true and proper worship. Do not conform to the pattern of this world, but be transformed by the renewing of

your mind. Then you will be able to test and approve what God's will is—his good, pleasing and perfect will (Rom. 12:1-2).

One thing about relationships is that they will constantly be developing. My wife and I have a great relationship, but does that mean that I am a perfect husband or that she is a perfect wife? No, of course not.

Does it mean our communication is perfect? No. Does it mean that we always understand and interpret one another correctly? No, it does not. What it does mean is that we are constantly striving to become closer to one another.

This is why the Bible gives us relational illustrations. We can understand how God views us and how we should view Him. If I go on a business trip away from my wife, does that mean we no longer have a relationship during that time simply because I am not physically with her? No, of course not.

Our relationships with one another are continual. God gave us these relational illustrations to help us understand how we are to view Christianity. It is not lone ritual that God wants; it is relationship. Notice the following texts:

> Rend your heart and not your garments. (Joel 2:13).

> For I desire mercy, not sacrifice, and acknowledgment of God rather than burnt offerings. (Hosea 6:6).

Once again, I ask: Does having a relationship with Jesus mean we can just live "any" way we want? Of course not! All relationships have boundaries. Besides, if we really care about God, we won't live just "any" way. If I love my wife, I won't treat her just "any" way. If I love my best friend, I won't treat him just "any" way. If I love my family, I won't treat them just "any" way.

Relationship is about caring for one another. It is about trying to please the other. It is about sacrificing for the other. No, it is not because of fear or obligation, but because of love and desire. In relationship, we find God and delight in His will (Psa. 119:47; 1 Jn. 5:3; 1 Cor. 10:31). It is in ritual where we lose God and forget what Christianity is all about.

God has always desired relationship with His creation. In ritual, my faith is placed in my accomplishments; in relationship, my faith is placed in Jesus. In ritual, my faith is placed in my knowledge; in relationship, my faith is placed in the all-knowing One. In ritual, my faith is placed in "me" getting everything right; in relationship, my faith is placed in the only One who could get it all right.

Ritual fails where Jesus prevails! In the next few chapters, I am going to discuss how this has changed my approach toward God, Scripture, and people.

CHAPTER 52
MY APPROACH TO GOD

When my framework changed, I started to make decisions based upon my love for Jesus. Instead of seeing Christianity as something I did, I began to realize being a Christian is who I am all the time.

I can't personally tell you enough about how much viewing Christianity through the proper framework of relationship has altered and deepened my whole Christian walk. It reminds me of the mindset Joseph had when he said to Potiphar's wife:

> How then could I do such a wicked thing and sin against God? (Gen. 39:9).

Joseph viewed his potential sin as one that would personally hurt God. No longer was it about what I could get away with. It wasn't about trying to find "legal loopholes" in the Bible. It was no longer about punching the clock or going through the motions.

Everything changed. I realized God wanted me to bring Him my heart. This is what God had always wanted. Notice the following passages:

> 'The multitude of your sacrifices—what are they to me?' says the Lord. 'I have more than enough of burnt offerings, of rams and the fat of fattened animals. I have no pleasure in the blood of bulls and lambs and goats.' (Isa. 1:11).

> You do not delight in sacrifice, or I would bring it; you do not take pleasure in burnt offerings. My sacrifice, O God, is a broken spirit; a broken and contrite heart you, God, will not despise. (Psa. 51:16-17).

Viewing Christianity through the lenses of a relationship changed everything for me. For the first time, I truly identified my problem. Before, God was a distant being who rewarded good works and punished bad works.

He was very impersonal in my mind. I had a very shallow and cold view of God. When I was infected with legalism, it was as if I worshipped and cared more about the Bible itself than I did God.

Jesus wasn't really in the picture as far as application was concerned. Now, all of that has changed. I revere God more than I ever have. I don't want to disappoint Him. No, it is not because of my fear of being lost, but because of my love for Him and my concern of hurting Him.

I think about my wife and how much I love her. I want to make her happy. I care about her so much. When I see her hurting, it hurts me. I want to be the best husband I know I can be to her because I love her. I now view Jesus Christ in a similar light. I want to make Him happy. He died for my sins.

When I started to focus on the actual message of the gospel, I couldn't help but love Jesus more than I ever had. Why would I want to hurt my best friend, especially when He only has my best interest in mind? It is no longer just about what I can do and what I can't do. It isn't just about finding loopholes. Instead, it is about doing everything I can to please Jesus Christ in my daily life.

CHAPTER 53
MY APPROACH TO SCRIPTURE

In a similar light, when I study Scripture, I no longer view the New Testament as a legal document. Keep in mind that the New Testament was still being written during the first century.

While we now have the totality of the New Testament to research and study, the early church might only hear the instructions when they were read in their assemblies (Col. 4:16). We have to be careful that we don't get so lost in knowledge that we can't find Jesus (1 Cor. 8:1; Jn. 5:39). I realized how I once approached the "law of Christ" was very similar to how the scribes and Pharisees approached the Old Law.

Thankfully, Jesus taught us how to understand Scripture and how to understand law. As I stated earlier, law, in and of itself, is not a bad thing. It is when we don't use it properly that it becomes wrong (1 Tim. 1:8).

Since we are to use the law properly, this means that we can also use the law improperly if we are not careful. We see examples of this found throughout Scripture. Jesus was particularly concerned with making sure people were using the law in a lawful manner. What does it mean to use the law in a lawful manner and how do I know if I am doing so?

Intrinsic in God's law has always been relational intelligence. In other words, His law must be looked at relationally. Jesus made this very clear when He was asked what the greatest command was. Here was His response:

'Love the Lord your God with all your heart and with all your soul and with all your mind.' This is the first and greatest commandment. And the second is like it: 'Love your neighbor as yourself.' All the Law and the Prophets hang on these two commandments' (Mt. 22:37-40).

Jesus taught that the way we view Scripture and biblical law is dependent upon loving God and loving people. When we read Scripture and law any other way, we are not properly approaching the Bible.

When I read and study the Scriptures, I must always read through the lenses of loving God and loving my neighbor. What does it look like when one fails to approach Scripture and law relationally?

One example can be found in Mk. 7:1-13. In this instance, the Jewish leaders were criticizing Jesus' disciples because they were eating with unwashed hands. During this time, it was customary for the Jews to ceremonially cleanse themselves.

This was not a part of the law of Moses but was a tradition that had been popularized in the Hebrew culture over the years. When the Pharisees and scribes noted that Jesus' disciples weren't conforming to this rabbinic tradition, they felt they had an indictment against Jesus and His disciples (Mk. 7:5).

Instead of Jesus entangling Himself in a frivolous debate over their tradition, He pointed out their hypocrisy and misuse of the law. You see, the law of Moses required the Jews to honor their parents. This included the idea of caring for them in their various needs (Mk. 7:10; Deut. 5:16).

Yet, some of the Jews had created a "legal loophole" in the law to excuse their responsibility to their parents. They would designate certain portions of their financial resources as "corban" (Mk. 7:11). Let me explain what that means.

The Greek word "korban" is related to the term "korbanas," which signifies the temple treasury offering.[65] The Jews had taken the word corban and coined it as a vow term.

One could designate their financial resources as corban as a way of reserving it, meaning that the money belonged to God and could not be used for personal interests. Jesus pointed out to these Jews that they had neglected their parental responsibility by an appeal to corban. He said:

> But you say that if anyone declares that what might have been used to help their father or mother is Corban (that is, devoted to God)— then you no longer let them do anything for their father or mother. Thus, you nullify the word of God by your tradition that you have handed down. And you do many things like that. (Mk. 7:11-13).

Jesus was rebuking them because the money that might have been used to provide for their aging parents was dedicated to the temple treasury. These Jews had found a way to justify their actions. Saying the money is "Corban" would exempt a person from his responsibility to his parents.

In other words, these Jews took a lawful Corban offering and used it in an unlawful and deceptive way to defraud their parents while gaining money for themselves. In very similar ways, I often found myself twisting my own traditions to justify what I wanted while condemning others.

In this instance, the scribes and Pharisees were guilty of leaving out relational intelligence when approaching the law. Thus, they failed to have a proper understanding of law which often led to a misapplication of it.

---

[65] http://biblehub.com/greek/2878a.htm. 2878a. korban; See also: *Wars 2.9.4*, Josephus.

In another example, Jesus' disciples were hungry and began to pluck heads of grain on the Sabbath (Mt. 12:1-8). The Pharisees had interpreted the Sabbath laws ritually instead of relationally (Deut. 23:25).

Once again, instead of Jesus involving himself in an endless back-and-forth debate about the specific Sabbath laws, Jesus taught them to view law through relationship. Notice the words of Jesus:

> He answered, 'Haven't you read what David did when he and his companions were hungry? He entered the house of God, and he and his companions ate the consecrated bread—which was not lawful for them to do, but only for the priests. Or haven't you read in the Law that the priests on Sabbath duty in the temple desecrate the Sabbath and yet are innocent? I tell you that something greater than the temple is here. If you had known what these words mean, 'I desire mercy, not sacrifice,' you would not have condemned the innocent. (Mt. 12:3-7).

Jesus alluded back to the example of David and his men eating the showbread when they were hungry and needed food (1 Sam. 21:1-9). The priests were the only ones who were supposed to eat the showbread (Mt. 12:4-5). David was not a priest.

Yet, he and his men still ate the showbread and were justified. In fact, even though the exception that Jesus alluded to is said to be just for the priests, there were also other exceptions in Lev. 22:11, 13.

Both Jesus and the priests in the days of David realized that there were other unstated exceptions to the rule. If they had no other means of getting bread, they could eat it. So too, David, without a means of getting bread for himself and his men, deserved the compassion of eating it. That is Jesus' whole point in Mt. 12:1-8.

Did this mean David and Jesus' disciples violated the law? Through the ritual lenses of the scribes and Pharisees, they did violate the law. Yet, law is not to be viewed ritually. Therefore, when properly understanding how to apply the law, we can see that

David and the disciples of Jesus did not violate the law. Jesus further proves this point in Mk. 2:27 when He says:

> The Sabbath was made for man, not man for the Sabbath. (Mk. 2:27).

The application of God's law can never contradict the purpose for which it was originally given. Therefore, if I am applying God's law in such a way that would contradict the actual purpose, I am no longer applying the law lawfully. Jesus said He is the one who gave the law (Mt. 12:8).

The law was made for man; man wasn't made for the law (Mk. 2:27). When we begin to treat the law with more love and respect than the people under the law, we have missed the very point of the law. Jesus ends His encounter here by saying:

> If you had known what these words mean, 'I desire mercy, not sacrifice,' you would not have condemned the innocent. (Mt. 12:7).

While many other examples could be listed, the aforementioned should be sufficient to show that we must view law through the lenses of relationship. I no longer approach Scripture as an attorney would approach a legal document. Jesus showed us that this is not how the Bible is to be understood.

The New Testament is not composed of legal documents; it is composed of love letters. Yes, there are still laws, restrictions, and regulations. However, we must learn to view those relationally instead of ritualistically. Our framework must hinge upon the two greatest commands of loving God and loving people (Mt. 22:37-40).

CHAPTER 54
MY APPROACH TO UNITY AND FELLOWSHIP

Viewing Christianity through the framework of law had failed me. The system had failed. Now, viewing God through the framework of relationship made perfect sense.

Viewing Scripture through relational intelligence made perfect sense. However, I was interested to see how this new framework would help me better understand my continual questioning of unity and fellowship.

In Chapter 28, I discussed my previous approach to unity and why it fails. Unfortunately, I had always been willing to declare "fellowship warfare" with other Christians because of disagreements about worship and other issues. I have seen these so-called "worship wars" take place over a wide range of subjects. The issues are limitless.

Instead of a peaceful and safe environment where Christians can come together and praise God in unity (Psa. 133:1), I had made the public worship service just another platform for division.

The public worship assembly had been a big part of my focus in my Christianity during that time. I would often preach on the importance of perfecting our worship assemblies to God.

It was as if we had easily accepted the fact that we couldn't live a perfect and sinless life the rest of the week, yet our worship had to be perfect and sinless. The majority of the divisions and debates in which I engaged had to do with subjective opinions about how to worship.

Some, if not most, of the things I believed about worship aren't necessarily wrong in and of themselves, but I would condemn other people if they failed to worship just like I worshipped. I was surprised to find that this isn't a new phenomenon.

In fact, in the Old Testament, there was a literal war that almost took place because of certain, well-intended Jews who thought they were defending the truth (Josh. 22:10-34).

When the sons of Reuben, Gad and the half-tribe of Manasseh came to the region of the Jordan, they built a large altar (Josh. 22:11). When the sons of Israel heard about this, they were ready to go to war against them, thinking they were in opposition to God (Josh. 22:12).

They weren't supposed to be building an altar and the sons of Israel were going to go and "set them straight." They accused the sons of Reuben, Gad, and the half-tribe of Manasseh of being unfaithful, turning away from God, and rebelling against the Lord since they had built an extra altar (Josh. 22:16). This sounded eerily familiar to how I acted toward those who disagreed with me.

However, Reuben, Gad, and the half-tribe of Manasseh explained to the sons of Israel that they had built this altar out of concern as a witness between them and their generations after them to show that they, too, have a portion in the Lord (Josh. 22:21-29).

They were not unfaithful to the Lord, nor had they rebelled against God. Fortunately, the sons of Israel realized the truth before starting an unnecessary war with Reuben, Gad, and the half tribe of Manasseh. The text says:

> They were glad to hear the report and praised God. And they talked no more about going to war against them to devastate the country where the Reubenites and the Gadites lived. (Josh 22:33).

It can also be the case that different church affiliations condemn one another because the other one doesn't do everything just like they do. In the New Testament, John tried to cause trouble because he saw someone casting out demons in Jesus' name who wasn't in their group.

John was proud of himself when he condemned the man since he didn't hang out with their specific group. Instead of Jesus patting John on the back and commending him, Jesus rebuked John. The text says:

> 'Master', said John, 'we saw someone driving out demons in your name and we tried to stop him, because he is not one of us.' 'Do not stop him,' Jesus said, 'for whoever is not against you is for you.' (Lk. 9:49-50).

It is so easy to condemn other churches simply because they don't worship the way we do or because they hold to different beliefs on various subjects. In fact, it is easy to condemn those within our own church affiliation or congregation when they don't agree with us.

However, instead of looking for any and every opportunity to wage warfare when we disagree with a brother or sister in Christ, the Scriptures teach that we should be constantly striving together for the faith of the gospel in one mind and spirit (Phil. 1:27; Rom. 14:19; Rom. 14:4; etc.).

I now realize that the reason I could never answer the question of unity and fellowship is because the question itself was predicated through the framework of legalism.

The idea of providing a universal list of issues considered "doctrine" and "non-doctrine" is a law-based approach. I felt like the rich young ruler who came to Jesus to ask Him what he needed to do to go to heaven, asking for the "list of essentials" (Mk. 10:17-20).

Jesus listed some things the man was already doing since He knew what was in the heart of this ruler. The man confidently told Jesus he was doing everything He listed. Then, Jesus did something that the man never saw coming. The text says:

> Jesus looked at him and loved him. 'One thing you lack,' he said. 'Go, sell everything you have and give to the poor, and you will have treasure in heaven. Then come, follow me.' (Mk. 10:21-22).

Can you imagine the shock that this rich young ruler must have felt when he heard Jesus' response? He may have had thoughts such as: Where is that command in the law? There is nothing in the Law of Moses that says you must go and sell everything you have and give the money to the poor. Where is the, "book, chapter, and verse" for that command?

Jesus made such a powerful point in this context. Here was a man who thought he had kept the "salvation issues," yet he failed because he missed the whole point.

Addressing the issue of Christian unity and fellowship through the framework of law will also fail – every single time. On the contrary, addressing the issue of unity and fellowship through the framework of relationship completely changes things.

We need to quit looking for a list that doesn't exist. If we are going to be successful in Christianity, we must put down the checklist and pick up our crosses (Lk. 9:23).

When we reduce Christianity to nothing more than a "list of essentials," we are taking away the very message that Jesus came to bring, which is to deny self and follow Him fully and completely (Lk. 9:23). The fact is that Christians will continue to grow (2 Pet. 3:18). Some Christians will be on spiritual milk while others will be on spiritual meat (Heb. 5:12-14).

The Bible teaches that a particular issue may cost one person their salvation, while not costing someone else their salvation. This would be based upon their heart, intent, knowledge, and current situation (2 Chron. 30:16-27).

I want to make it clear that I am not saying that lines shouldn't be drawn at times. Just like with any relationships, boundaries are necessary. Whether we admit it or not, everyone draws lines. However, based upon my experience, here is what I found are the main five problems:

1. Drawing lines among other believers where God hasn't draw them.
2. Believing that it is better to draw too many lines than not enough.
3. Being inconsistent on how we pick and choose the issues over which to divide.
4. Failing to take the proper biblical protocol when drawing lines.
5. Condemning the eternal fate of others when we draw lines.

Most lines that believers draw among other believers are not lines found in Scripture. They are not lines God has drawn. As we learned from Paul earlier, we can disagree on many things. Paul taught that being wrong on a subject or topic is not the same thing as being in sin. Otherwise, we would all have to claim absolute knowledge and infallibility on every single topic. Such is impossible.

Therefore, we have to be careful that we are not calling something a sin unless God has called it a sin. If someone is not violating God's law (Rom. 4:15; 1 Jn. 3:4), we have no right to tell someone they are in sin.

May we kindly disagree with them? Absolutely (Acts 15:36-41). Might they be wrong? Sure (1 Cor. 8:1-13). However, unless they are violating God's law, they are not in sin. A lot of division will immediately cease when we realize that we are drawing lines where God never drew them.

It is also important to keep in mind that we will be judged based upon the lines we draw (Mt. 7:1-5). Where I once believed it was better to draw too many lines than not enough, I am now under the persuasion that it is better to draw fewer lines since the Bible teaches we should always err on the side of mercy instead of judgment (Ja. 2:13; Mt. 7:1-2).

We also need to make sure we are being consistent. I found that my standard of drawing lines through the framework of law was not only unbiblical, but impossible to uphold consistently. I was getting to the point where I couldn't even fellowship myself on most days.

When we do draw lines, we must personally make sure we are being consistent with how we do so and that we are drawing lines in such a way that is biblical and reasonable.

However, what happens if we are fully convinced someone is not just wrong, but they are violating God's law and we feel it is necessary to draw lines? At this point, if we believe we must act, then we should follow the proper steps and biblical protocol.

This involves going to the person in humility and trying to help them overcome their sin (Mt. 18:15-18; 2 Tim. 2:24-26; Gal. 6:1). A gracious amount of time striving to help that person should be given. The Bible gives no timeline. Therefore, we shouldn't either. Only those directly involved in the situation should be the ones who make the determination based upon mercy, truth, wisdom, and love.

If no change or improvement has been made and you still believe a line must be drawn, then when you draw your line, you should never view those believers as enemies (2 Thess. 3:15; 1 Cor. 5). Instead, we should be respectful and kind toward them as we admonish them and pray that God will look to their hearts and forgive them.[66]

Finally, once lines are drawn, it is not up to us to judge the eternal fate of individuals. We would all do much better if we focused more on improving ourselves instead of constantly trying to figure out the fate of everyone else.

Remember the story of Hezekiah and the Jews in 2 Chron. 30? If I were the judge, they never would have had a chance. They were violating the law. Yet, God's grace covered them because God looked to their hearts. It is never my job to judge someone's eternal fate. Notice the following verses:

> Make it your ambition to lead a quiet life: You should mind your own business... (1 Thess. 4:11).

> There is only one Lawgiver and Judge, the one who is able to save and destroy. But you--who are you to judge your neighbor? (Ja. 4:12).

> Who are you to judge someone else's servant? To their own master, servants stand or fall. And they will stand, for the Lord is able to make them stand. (Rom. 14:4).

At the end of the day, we must all ascertain situations and make decisions the best we can based upon our own conviction and conscience knowing that we will be judged for how we did so (Phil. 2:12; Rom. 14:23; Jn. 7:24). Here are five points to which I believe we should adhere when addressing unity and fellowship through the lenses of relationship. Before I draw a spiritual line of fellowship with a brother or sister, I should make sure:

1. I am thoroughly convinced I am drawing a line where God drew His line (and I am ready to give an account for it).

2. I am giving more mercy than judgment and erring on the side of mercy.

3. I am being as consistent as I can with how I am drawing my lines.

---

[66] Ezek. 22:30; 2 Chron. 30:18-20; Eph. 4:32

4. I have the proper attitude and protocol when approaching this individual or situation.

5. I am allowing God to be the ultimate judge for the person's eternal fate.

PART 13: CONCLUSION

CHAPTER 55
ALREADY LEFT LEGALISM?

This book was written with three different groups of people in mind:

1. Those who have already left legalism in some form or fashion.
2. Those who are in the process of leaving legalism.
3. Those who are thinking about leaving legalism/those who are interested in considering a different perspective.

As we are nearing the end of the book, I would like to address all three of these groups. To those who have already left legalism, I want to caution you that we should continue to evaluate ourselves and to make sure we are "practicing what we are preaching."

When I figured out this system change in my life just as you did, I noticed that I was still failing to practice what I preached. When I started to write blog articles about my change, I would receive criticism and "hate mail" from old friends or old contemporaries.

Instead of being the bigger person and actually practicing what I was preaching, I would retaliate just like the "old Kevin." I wasn't using everything I learned about mercy and grace. I wasn't taking the relational approach to things.

I say all of that to say this is a very difficult thing to do and I still fail often. My love for others, especially my enemies, is not yet where it needs to be, but I am working on it daily.

Since for so many years my automatism was to attack people when they attacked me, I have to fight diligently against that mentality. At one time, I assumed the worst in others. Therefore, I still find myself doing the same thing more than I care to admit.

I have learned through this experience that law-system Christianity is so much easier to live than relational Christianity. That is why so many Jews rejected Jesus and why so many Christians today choose to remain in legalism. It is much easier.

Telling people that they are wrong when they disagree with you? That is easy. Causing division? Anybody can do that. Striving for unity despite disagreements? That is difficult.

Lashing out in a discussion when somebody has attacked you? Easy. Holding back and showing love instead? Difficult. When people treat you with judgment, judge them back? Very easy. Showing them grace and mercy? Very hard.

Taking the grace road is always the way to go with people. I try to explain this to others. Some get it and others do not. This is another one of those counterintuitive approaches again.

Here is what I have discovered: You cannot debate somebody into grace. They have to be shown grace. They have to experience it. If someone is completely opposed to the idea of reconsidering the way they are doing Christianity, then this book will not do that person any good and neither will a Facebook debate or mocking them.

How can we ever help someone find the grace that we once didn't understand if we aren't showing it to them in love and mercy? Trust me, I know. I was there for many years. It didn't matter what I read or with whom I spoke. At that point, I was still "watching the video with the wrong audio" as I explained earlier.

Until someone is at the point of questioning, re-examining, or, as in my case, seeing that what I was doing doesn't work, then they won't change. However, instead of responding with hate and bitterness, we need to respond in love and mercy. Please, never forget this. Let's hold each other accountable because if we do not, we, too, will fail.

Please, let us not be arrogant in the freedom we have found. Do not look down upon those sitting in the seats we once occupied. It is easy to do. I know. I often wonder how I could have fallen for such a warped and faulty system. Yet, if I did, then I should understand that others have, and will also.

If the hurt from those in the past is too great, remember the pain Jesus suffered. Also, remember the pain your legalism also caused others at one point.

Out of everyone living, we should have the most empathy toward those infected with legalism. Similar to how a surviving cancer patient in remission should have the most understanding toward cancer patients, so we should have the most understanding for those struggling in legalism.

CHAPTER 56

IN THE PROCESS OF LEAVING LEGALISM?

This chapter is written for those who have already made the decision to leave legalism and are in the process. Right now, you are going through unimaginable pain. Depending upon your situation, you could be losing friends, your job, and even family.

For me personally, leaving legalism meant leaving my job. It also resulted in me losing friendships with my mentor (Mr. Williams), a co-worker (Mike), and the majority of my acquaintances at that time. I didn't want to lose those friendships, but in order for them to remain intact, I would have had to continue to believe something I no longer believed.

I made it clear that I wanted to remain friends. They made it clear that they didn't since my belief had changed. I told them I could still fellowship them despite our disagreements. However, they told me that they no longer believed they could fellowship me because of our disagreements.

By the way, on a side note, they still fellowship people with whom they disagree. This is the inconsistency and postmodernism I mentioned earlier.

Mike told me at the time that he didn't have a problem associating with me as long as it didn't conflict with his current job position at his church. As soon as it did, he disassociated with me. This shows not only the inconsistency, but the politics and hypocrisy that legalism has created as I have also already discussed in detail.

Perhaps you are questioning if all of this is worth it. Is the sacrifice you are going through worth it in the end? Let me tell you that it is. As someone who lost my own identity, my job, my friends, and my purpose, it was the absolute best thing that could have happened to me during that time. In losing everything, I truly found Jesus.

You will need to understand that it will likely continue to get much worse before it gets better. I don't know your specific situation, but I have personally spoken to hundreds of people who have left legalism. You are not alone. One preacher told me that he realized he could no longer be involved in legalism.

When this happened, he was fired from his job and his whole family, to this day, has refused to have any contact with him for over two years now. This includes his sisters, his brothers-in-law, his parents, and his grandparents.

However, the more I learned about how this man responded, the more I saw what grace in action looks like. Instead of firing back, this man still sends flowers to his mother on Mother's Day and still writes cards to his family letting them know how much he loves them.

By the way, all of this occurred because he said he was no longer going to condemn other Christians just because they didn't worship exactly like he did. He hasn't even changed how he worships; he simply stated that he wasn't going to condemn other Christians for worshipping differently than him. It was for this reason this man lost his job and relationships with most of his family.

I know it is tough. The man in the story above knows it is tough. The countless others who have left legalism know how tough it is to leave it behind. Please, do not give up on freedom. Do not turn back to spiritual bondage (Gal. 1:6-10).

As you are going through this change, I beg that you, too, show mercy and grace to those around you. I didn't do that when I first changed. I greatly regret it. I was very ugly to people at first and I missed out on a big opportunity.

You want to keep the doors of opportunity open to others in the future. Keep in mind that even though you may not think that other people are questioning the bonds of legalism, they are paying attention to your behavior and your change and that could impact them down the road.

If they see an actual change in you and can tell that things are different, then it will make an impact. I can promise you that. Just remember to be the person you are telling others you are. It is something I still have to work on every day.

CHAPTER 57
THINKING ABOUT LEAVING LEGALISM?

This chapter is for those who are thinking about leaving legalism. You have such a special place in my heart right now because I know where you are. It is terrifying. It is horrifying. This was the worst and best time in my life. It was the worst time in the present and it has become the best time in my past.

You may be a teenager reading this book because your father is a preacher at a church and you have been questioning things.

You, yourself, might be the preacher at a church and you realize what this change would mean and you are counting the cost. Perhaps your spouse has completely bought into the framework of law and you are starting to see the fallacies.

Maybe you are like one person who e-mailed me who was an atheist and who found a legalistic church that appeared to have all the answers. Yet, when studying further, he saw the inconsistencies and started to doubt the existence of God again.

I actually have had two friends who were very dedicated to their (legalistic) Christianity, yet they saw the inconsistency and blamed it on the Bible instead of questioning their framework.

The bottom line is that I don't know your situation, but I understand it. Let me tell you the good news. You can change and things will get better. Yes, it will be a long road.

For some, it will be longer than others because it will depend upon how deep the hole is that you have dug for yourself. However, you are never too far gone.

If you are reading this, then you are at least willing to consider an alternative. This already proves you are not too far gone in your thinking. This already shows you are open to hearing something different. If you are questioning the idea of leaving legalism, then know that it will be a very difficult process - both internally and externally.

It can be a hard transition internally because your brain, like mine, has been trained (perhaps for years) to operate through a faulty framework. It took my emotional brain over a year to finally catch up with my logical brain.

Logically, I saw where I had been wrong and how I had been approaching God and Scripture incorrectly. Yet, emotionally I was still stuck feeling the way I had always felt. This is when I like to remind people to trust in God and not their own feelings (Prov. 3:5-6; 18:2). John said:

> If our hearts condemn us, we know that God is greater than our hearts, and he knows everything. (1 Jn. 3:20).

Feelings are very deceptive and people will attempt to manipulate you and use your feelings against you. Don't let them. There can also be a lot of regret and remorse. Once again, this will depend upon how legalistic you were and how legalism manifested itself in your life.

Since I was very harsh toward others in the name of Jesus, I really carried a lot of guilt at first. After asking God to forgive my stupid, sinful ways, I started to try to contact everyone I could to apologize to them. I then realized I couldn't even remember all of the people I hurt.

I overcame this by understanding that God has forgiven me. I thought of all the people Paul hurt in his former life, yet he moved forward knowing that he had been forgiven. If you experience guilt and remorse, don't beat yourself up. Instead, use that to motivate you to help others.

Aside from the internal transition, there will be a lot of external factors you will face. As I have already mentioned, I have personally known many preachers who have lost their preaching jobs because they decided they were no longer going to bind man-made laws.

I know many people who have had their own parents, siblings, and grandparents withdraw from/excommunicate them because they decided to leave legalism. Depending upon your church affiliation, you may even be harassed and shamed.

Everyone's transition out of legalism is going to look different, with some suffering more than others. It has never been easy for anyone. I say all of this to let you know the reality of the situation. It is often difficult to even question legalism without being automatically "marked" by others who are caught up in legalism.

You may have even bought this book in secret because you don't want anyone to know that you are reading it. Trust me, I understand this very well. If this is where you find yourself, please know that I am willing to personally speak with you in confidence and connect you with others with whom you can speak in confidence as well. We are all here to help one another and I can connect you to a large network of individuals.

Since I have changed, I have been contacted by a plurality of Christians, including preachers and even professors at Christian schools telling me that they are in the process of questioning legalism, but they need encouragement.

Some are afraid because of their families and friends. Others are fearful of losing their jobs at schools and churches. Some are afraid purely out of all the pressure. As you change, please know that there are many who will be there for you to talk with in a safe and confidential environment.

CHAPTER 58
FINDING YOUR OWN FAITH

It is my prayer and hope that you've enjoyed the book and that it has given you many "aha" moments that will propel you forward. As I conclude this book, I would like to once again say thank you so much for taking the time to read it.

I would like to encourage you to make sure that you develop your own faith. Legalism really feeds off of "group thinking." This is a phycological phenomenon.

> Groupthink occurs when a group with a particular agenda makes irrational or problematic decisions because its members value harmony and coherence over accurate analysis and critical evaluation. Individual members of the group are strongly discouraged from any disagreement with the consensus and set aside their own thoughts and feelings to unquestioningly follow the word of the leader and other group members. In a groupthink situation, group members refrain from expressing doubts, judgments or disagreement with the consensus.[67]

If this sounds even remotely similar to your "faith," then you probably don't actually have your own personal faith. The fact that I used to even mock the idea of a personal relationship with Jesus shows how indoctrinated I was in "groupthink" ideology. Make sure that whatever your faith is, it is your own faith. Your relationship with Christ is predicated upon your own faith. It is not predicated upon your family, your preacher, your church affiliation, or the congregation you attend.

---

[67] www.psychologytoday.com/us/basics/groupthink

Regardless of where you are in your journey (especially as it relates to questioning or leaving legalism), I want to leave you with some "do's and don'ts" that I pray will be beneficial:

Don't believe you have to defend yourself. There are going to be people who want to talk to you to try and bring you back to their belief system. If you believe that the conversation could be beneficial for both of you, then please engage in a Christ-like way.

However, if it is someone who is only wanting to condemn you or "correct you," then please do not believe you have to defend yourself. Often those conversations turn into pointless debates that can harm rather than help (2 Tim. 2:23-24; Titus 3:9; Prov. 26:4).

Always show kindness. It is not enough to theologically leave legalism. We must also practically leave legalism in our actions (1 Jn. 3:18). I want to really reinforce this idea. This means that we must show others the grace and mercy that was and is shown to us through Jesus Christ.

People will attack you. Don't attack back. People will condemn you. Don't condemn them. I fell for these tactics at first. I later learned that grace and mercy will always win. People will get personal with you. Don't get personal with them. Learn to live in grace and mercy.

Be careful to make sure you want to change and not just change sides. When I first found true freedom in Christ, I didn't really change. I changed sides, but I didn't actually change. I was informed, but I wasn't transformed (Rom. 12:1-2). I was still very judgmental toward those still involved in legalism. I became arrogant toward those in legalism.

We need to realize that others are still in spiritual bondage, most likely for the same reasons you were. Think of yourself. Remember you were once in bondage. Be patient and do not condemn them, but show them mercy, grace, and love.

Accept the fact that legalism is everywhere. Legalism is not just in one church. I can't emphasize this enough. Legalism is a framework for viewing everything else. There will be people everywhere infected with legalism.

I am aware that there are different levels of legalism among individuals and there are certainly some church affiliations that cater to and enable legalism more than others. However, remember that legalism and its effects can be found anywhere.

Don't blame God for bad theology. Unfortunately, as I discussed earlier, I had two friends become atheists because they blamed God for the legalism they were taught. They bought into the legalistic system for so long that they dismissed the whole Bible because of their own bad theology. Legalism is bad theology. Legalism is not from God. Please don't blame God.

Don't be a victim. It is natural to grieve when coming out of legalism, especially if leaving legalism severs relationships with family or friends. However, don't become a victim of your past circumstances. Even if you were a victim, you don't have to be any longer. It is time to take responsibility for your own belief now and quit blaming others for your past.

Instead of holding grudges and being bitter, remind yourself that you have a different appreciation for the freedom in Christ than those who never had to experience legalism. It is important to move forward in your Christian walk without bitterness and resentment.

Leaving legalism isn't easy, but the freedom that awaits is well worth it. As I conclude my time with you, I would like to summarize the key points of this book and pray that you will consider them as you continue your journey:

1. The proper understanding of legalism is simply the belief that salvation can be gained through good works/a law system.

2. Unlike immorality or blatant rebellion, legalism is a different kind of spiritual poison because it often appears under the guise of righteousness.

3. Legalism is a framework, a mindset, and an approach. The specific doctrines and actions in which it can manifest itself are literally limitless. Be careful that you don't just deal with the symptoms of legalism, but that you deal with legalism itself.

4. Legalism can be found anywhere, with any church affiliation, and with any person.

5. In this book, it has been my objective to deal with legalism as a concept. I have attempted to keep the focus on dealing with the actual "poison" itself.

6. In order to overcome legalism in all areas of your life, your framework must change. It must become relational and not legal.

While the road ahead may be difficult, realize freedom is waiting for you, and Jesus holds the key. Many Christians who knew me before I changed told me that they never thought I would find freedom.

Some told me that I was the most legalistic Christian they had ever met. That is good news for you! Do you want to know why? The reason it is good news is because if God can change me, He can certainly change you, too!

I want to be here for you any way I can. I believe God allowed me to go through what I did in order to appreciate spiritual freedom and help others find it.

I need your help, however. I am trying to spread the truth about legalism and freedom to as many people as I can and I hope you'll help spread the word with me.

Here are a couple of simple things you can do to help me and others. If you enjoyed the book, please leave a review of the book on Amazon and share it with others. Just go to your order history, find the book, and then leave a review.

You can also search for the book and hit the "write a review" button. Please share the book with others by telling them about it and sharing it on your social media.

This will help support and encourage other people who are suffering or have suffered from legalism. People who are going through a transition will feel less alone when reading your review. Hopefully, thanks to you, they will find the courage to do something about it.

On the other hand, if you didn't like the book for some reason, then please reach out to me directly at kevin@kevinpendergrass.com. I value your feedback, even if it is negative. While I am not always able to respond to every e-mail, I personally try to read all of my e-mails and take the things said into consideration.

Please connect with me and other Christians on social media to discuss this book:

https://www.facebook.com/adifferentkindofpoison
https://www.facebook.com/fortheloveofthetruth

For further study material and to stay connected, you can visit my blog:

http://www.kevinpendergrass.com

Regardless of your situation, please know that what you tell me will stay confidential. I am not here to judge your situation, but to do what I can to help rid you of this nasty poison that I had in my veins for years. Remember, freedom is waiting if you're willing. Never forget what following God is all about:

Act justly and to love mercy and to walk humbly with your God. (Mic. 6:8).

May God bless you!

Kevin Pendergrass
kevinpendergrass.com
kevin@kevinpendergrass.com